15/

FRENCH ORIGINAL ENGRAVINGS
FROM MANET TO THE PRESENT TIME

THIS VOLUME, EDITED BY ANDRÉ
GLOECKNER, WAS FIRST PUBLISHED IN
SEPTEMBER MCMXXXIX BY THE HYPERION
PRESS, PARIS. COLOUR PLATES ENGRAVED
BY ÉTABLISSEMENTS JEAN MALVAUX,
BRUSSELS, PRINTED BY G. LANG, PARIS.
TEXT PRINTED BY G. DESGRANDCHAMPS,
PARIS. PHOTOGRAVURE BY M. FRANÇOIS,
LIMOGES. BINDING BY J. TAUPIN, PARIS.

FRENCH
ORIGINAL ENGRAVINGS
FROM MANET
TO THE PRESENT TIME

BY

CLAUDE ROGER-MARX

THE HYPERION PRESS
LONDON — PARIS — NEW YORK
MCMXXXIX

I. – THE REVIVAL OF COPPER ENGRAVING CIRCA 1862

FOUNDATION OF THE SOCIETY OF ETCHERS

Our subject is so vast that certain limits must be imposed from the outstart. The word " engraving " we shall take in its widest significance — that is to say to cover engravings on wood, copper and stone — and we shall begin by excluding all engravings which are reproductions of other artists' subjects, however great their interest may be. Our study is confined to French engravers, and by French we mean those who have worked mainly in France, such as Jongkind, Mary Cassatt, or Picasso. Others like Seymour Haden, Whistler and Ensor we shall consider as belonging to their country of origin, though we are fully aware that such discrimination must in many cases be arbitrary. Moreover, it is not Manet himself whom we shall take as our starting-point, but that great movement for the revival of the original print which came to a head in France towards 1862.

After that golden age of lithography which saw the masterpieces of Géricault, Delacroix and Barye, and the charming prints of Charlet, Decamps, Isabey, and Gavarni, the practice of stone engraving was practically abandoned in the middle of the XIXth century with the solitary exception of one great master, Honoré Daumier. Etching, too, fell into abeyance. Only a few impressions were made of Chasseriau's *Othello* (1884). Daubigny and Charles Jacques alone squandered their talent on little pictures in which refined sentiment was combined with minuteness of execution.

A forerunner of Millet and Legros, Charles Jacques sensed the majesty of rustic types and works. In the skies and country landscapes of Daubigny flickered the lights which heralded the coming of Impressionism. Corot had as yet presented his friends with only one or two samples of his burin, all of them of little importance. Millet, on the other hand, had already engraved several big plates; against the background of an immense landscape, cut with the sharp, striking lines of his impulsive and passionate design, a number of admirable silhouettes are portrayed tilling the soil with priestly solemnity. Paris was the subject which for twenty years had been monopolising the work of Charles Méryon, but the persecution mania to which he eventually succumbed was already showing itself in his exaggerated treatment of the incoherent types which now appeared on his otherwise perfect prints. There were several others who had practised engraving in their spare moments, notably that charming coxcomb Adolphe Hervier. All these endeavours, however, were generally regarded with indifference. Wood-cutting alone, saved by the skill of the interpreters of Gustave Doré, enjoyed some credit with the public.

It was at this point that a kind of conspiracy, hitherto without parallel, was

7

set on foot to infuse some of its old vitality into the art of original engraving. What were the sources and origins of this movement ? Who was its leader ? Was it Legros ? Was it Bracquemond ? Painters, poets, printers and editors all strove together without ulterior motives, as though they were all genuinely convinced that the future of art as a whole was at stake. One by one, Théophile Gautier, Charles Baudelaire and Burty made their mighty voices heard, while latent talent was roused to activity by Bracquemond, who had known the smell of printer's ink from childhood and for whom the craft held no secrets. In his writings and by his spoken word, quite regardless of all personal interest, he sounded the praises of the " multiplied design ". At a time when the burin, the etching or the wood-cut was looked upon solely as the means of reproducing — and as often as not of muti-lating — the masterpieces of the past, these great pioneers, took up the cause of *original engraving*. They had the good fortune of enlisting the support of Delâtre, a printer brought up in an art school, and Cadart, a publisher whose courageous face — portrayed in turn by Desboutins and Ribot — reflected his readiness to subordinate the immediate prospects of success to the love of struggling for a fine cause.

It is astonishing to read the list of collaborators whom the *Society of Etchers* united or strove to unite. Manet, Daumier, Jongkind, Legros, Fantin-Latour, Seymour Haden, Ribot, Whistler, Degas, Pissarro, Puvis de Chavannes, Courbet, Eugène Boudin, together with a number of lesser talents, were called upon to add to the glory of French art. Many of them were then only on the threshold of their careers.

Ever since, whenever the art of engraving has found itself in danger, it has always been saved by a conspiracy of painters and writers. In every case it has been the concerted efforts of an *élite* which have helped it to surmount material obstacles, to survive the ephemeral discouragement of artists, publishers, and dealers. Throughout the XIXth and the XXth centuries it was Théophile Gautier, Baudelaire, Bracquemond, Burty, Goncourt, Buhot, Guérard, Roger Marx, Auguste Lepère, and Ambroise Vollard who from time to time helped to revive failing energy, to break away from the dead letter of routine, and to avert the various perils caused by economic conditions or aggravated by professional errors. In the mean-time the struggle continued more fiercely than ever between the specialists who claimed to be the sole guardians of the secrets of true technique, and the *painter-engravers* who, from their very first attempts, eclipsed the specialists who initiated them in their art.

For all the masterly skill of Bracquemond, which is so strikingly apparent in the charming plates which combine the heritage of the Western masters with that of Japan (*Le Vieux Cos, Le haut d'un battant de porte*, and the *Portrait of Edmond de Goncourt*), we cannot help feeling an even greater admiration for that constant presence of spirit and the vigorous intelligence which he never fails to apply to every domain of his activity. As an engraver he is still a slave of his craft, but he becomes its master in his discourses and his writings, where the requirements of good design and lucid composition are set forth in a language which may at times be diffuse, but which is nevertheless in the constant service of a courageous and clear idea.

We shall not attempt in our present study to conceal our preference for the work of the *painter-engravers*. One can be a master at using the burin's point on a polished plate, at getting the maximum effect from the printing qualities of copper, at producing a perfect print from the point of view of execution, without at the same time having anything to express. This, unfortunately, is so often the case with many virtuosos, who affect an unbounded contempt for the painter-engravers, considering them to be no better than untutored apprentices ignorant of style. And yet it was the masters and the painters, as Bracquemond pointed out, who " created the true school of engraving, while engravers as such never faced the problem of regularising and perfecting those means which the painters had discovered. There is no portrait engraver who has shown greater mastery in placing his figures than Van Dyck; we know of no architectural engraver who has surpassed Canaletto or Piranese, no landscape engraver who has produced better studies of work in the fields than Claude or Ruysdael. None of these masters have looked upon engraving solely from the point of view of the actuel process of production; they all designed and made their prints in the same spirit in which they painted their pictures. "

We could have quoted these lines in the very beginning of our introduction, for they are in the nature of a manifesto. They represent, too, the point of view which Gautier and Baudelaire expressed in the first publications of the Society of Etchers, soon after its foundation in 1862. The *Souvenir of Italy* by Corot, the *Unknown*, *Vannaux*, and *Sarcelles* by Bracquemond, the *Sheep in the Park* by Daubigny, *The Refectory* and *The Riding-School* by Legros, *The Gypsies* by Manet, the *View of Maasluis* by Jongkind, the *View of the Thames* by Seymour Haden, the *Barges at Low Tide* by Hervier, and *The Prayer* by Ribot are the outstanding features of the symposium produced by Delâtre in collaboration with Cadart. Gautier supplied a preface remarkable for the directness with which it conveys its ardent message. " Every etching, " he wrote, " is an original drawing. Success, however, can only be achieved by a steady hand, a firmness of touch and a foreknowledge of result which are not always to be found among the honest and the painstaking. There can be no fumbling, no retouching, no alteration. There is nothing finite or laboured about an etching. It never belies the simplicity of the spirit in which it was conceived. It conveys its meaning by a hint, by a suggestion.... If any of these plates appear in your judgment to be harsh or truculent, you should not forget that it is in the nature of every reaction to go to extremes, that the Society of Etchers has been founded precisely with the object of combatting that automatic routine which cramps the work and disfigures the true ideas of the artist, and that it is the intention of its founders to speak directly to the public through the medium of their plates, at their own risk and peril."

In the *Boulevard*, Baudelaire summed up the situation with that keen insight and lightning precision which are characteristic of all his writings :

" The discredit and indifference into which the noble art of engraving has fallen is, alas, only too apparent. It is only by turning over the leaves of old folios of the past that we can grasp the splendid qualities of the burin. But there is one genre which has fallen into even deeper oblivion than the burin : I speak of etching. The truth is that this type of art, so subtle and so superb, so simple and yet so profound, so gay and yet so severe, a type which, paradoxically, can unite qualities most diverse and express so well the personal character of the artist, has never enjoyed much popularity with the common multitude. Indeed, apart from the prints of Rembrandt, who is there who really cares for the etching ? Who, apart from collectors, is aware of all the different forms of perfection which can be achieved in this type that has come down to us from past ages ? The XVIIIth century had an abundance of charming etchings. They can be found for ten sous, hidden away in dusty files, where often for many years they wait for the touch of a familiar hand. " Is not Baudelaire pointing out the path on which the Goncourt brothers were to tread ? The poet then goes on to forestall a number of objections and to denounce the dangers which lie in store for those who, for lack of a sure technique, might fall into the errors of slipshod and incorrect ways, indecision, lack of finish, and faulty execution. " I can foresee that many will derive the same kind of vanity from their audacity as the slovens who think that their untidiness is a sign of independence. When men whose talent is mature and profound take the public into their confidence by revealing their roughly sketched plates, all is well and good, for they have a right to do so. The crowd of imitators, however, can become too numerous. In conclusion, one should not forget that etching is an art as dangerous as it is profound, full of snares; and that it lays bare the defects of the spirit as clearly as its good qualities. And, like every great art, exceedingly complex in its apparent simplicity, it exacts a long vigil of devotion before it allows itself to be led to perfection. "

To hear Baudelaire expressing himself in so decisive a manner, one might imagine that it was posterity itself that was picking and choosing among the works which were to be brought together in the publications of the Society of Etchers, pronounced this or that plate by Méryon to be a masterpiece and welcomed the publication of the *Views of Holland* by Jongkind, of the *Book of Etchings* by Manet, of this or that series by Hervier or Daubigny, or of the notable work of Delacroix which, after a lapse of nearly thirty years, introduces the author of the *Women of Algiers* under an aspect hitherto almost unknown. At the same time as Baudelaire and Gautier, Burty denounced the injustices of official hanging committees, and urged engravers to form an independent society and isolate themselves as completely as possible from all administrative guidance. He protested against the perilous ways of Gustave Doré and his interpreters, who were robbing the wood-cut of its simplicity; he deplored the decadence of lithographic art and the death of the burin. He encouraged the renascence of the etching " handled by young artists full of taste and vigour ", while warning them against certain crudities of style and reminding them that " an impression of the whole can be united with precision in execution. " His enthusiasm did not blind him to the fact that, after a number of years had elapsed, the good in Cadart's publications was beginning to be submerged by the mediocre. Against the colourless imitators of Corot he held up the pith and strength of character of Whistler, Seymour Haden, or Corot himself. It was he who, in 1869, suggested to Manet, Millet, Corot and Jongkind that they should illustrate *Sonnets and Etchings*.

The activity of Cadart, which was not confined to engravings on copper, continued undaunted by any of the difficulties that stood in its way. In 1868 the *Society of Etchers* became *The New Illustration*. This publication, which lasted for thirteen years, introduced several interesting recruits, such as Buhot and Desboutin, adding their names to those of Jongkind, Bracquemond, Daubigny, Bonvin, Ribot, etc. It was mostly the same names, too, that appeared in *The Modern Etching*, a parallel publication which came out from 1874 to 1881. In his famous prefaces Burty recalled the part which had been played by the great forerunners, Delacroix, Barye, and Méryon, stimulated the zeal of amateurs by extolling the charm of the " perfect print," and approached, one by one, the problems of paper, ink and impression. Unfortunately the cause which he was pleading became more and more difficult to defend. Etching had been taken up by a number of competent artists, but they contented themselves with vulgarising the inspiration of Méryon and Corot. Le Rat and Laleuze fell into a groove of laboured illustration; the work of Chifflard was burdened with a heavy romanticism; Carolus Duran and Detaille derived little profit from their incursions into the field of engraving. Moreover, the impressions produced at Delâtre's printing-works ended up by becoming a mere formula : the subject was lost in too wide a setting, and the finished productions owed more to the artifices of the printer than to the design itself. Here again, Burty pointed out how dangerous it is for the artist to become too openly dependent on the printer's skill : " Do not cite Rembrandt as an instance. The engraver who makes his own prints continues his own work. He is free to choose his process. It is a very different matter when the engraver entrusts his plate to a printer. All the tones of the engraved picture must already be contained in the metal, and when the printer is expected to achieve that which the artist alone has the knowledge and ability to provide, and whose duty it is to provide it, then it is an admission of failure on the part of the artist. "

Nothing could be added to this clear definition of the conflict which recurred again and again between those who maintained that the print should be taken " as it comes " and those who indulged their fancy by trying to make every print an independent work of art, differentiated by variations in the process of inking. The latter conception may only be admitted as legitimate in the case of those artists who were their own printers, such as Whistler, Buhot and Forain.

Bracquemond, without entirely refusing to collaborate, soon dissociated himself from publications whose guiding spirit he had ceased to be. The painter-engravers suffered a rapid disappointment, and directed their efforts to other channels. From 1874 onwards most of them found in the Impressionist exhibitions masters, such as Degas, who had not taken any part in Cadart's publications, and who had so far only engraved in private for their own personal satisfaction.

Little has been written about that publication, entitled : *Night and Day* — the dream of Degas, Pissarro, Mary Cassatt, and Raffaelli — of which only one issue appeared in 1880 in the Rue des Pyramides. It contained such masterpieces as *At the Louvre* by Degas and *The Undergrowth at the Hermitage* by Pissarro. In view of the indifference of the public, however, this venture was not continued any further. There is little doubt that *Night and Day* might have attracted such colla-borators as Legros, who had for a long time been settled in England, Manet, who was soon after to abandon graphic art owing to the scanty success which his plates had enjoyed, and many of the leaders of the Impressionist movement — Renoir, Sisley, Monet or Cézanne — who at that period, had circumstances been more favourable, would have succumbed, like Pissarro, to the lure of the metal. They would no doubt have been joined, too, by those who were marked as potential lithographers or etchers by the quality of their draughtsmanship, men like Constan-tin Guys, who was an engraver without knowing it. As it was, the art of engraving passed through a barren period about 1880. Apart from Legros and Degas, it was redeemed only by Rodolphe Bresdin and Buhot, two solitary alchemists, and by Auguste Rodin, whose admirable dry-points were only to be appreciated at a considerably later date. The only branch of engraving which enjoyed a certain prestige was the engraving of interpretation, in which we note the work of Flameng, Jacquemart, Chauvel, Weltner, and above all, by Claude Gaillard, that magnificent follower of the XVIIth century portrait painters. For reasons which often had little to do with art, the admiration of writers was wasted on the work of Felicien Rops, saturated with libertine and diabolical pretensions.

After this brief outline of the progress of original etching over a period of twenty years, we may now approach the work of Manet and his contemporaries : Degas, Legros, Corot, Jongkind, and Bresdin.

THE ENGRAVINGS OF DEGAS

The name of Degas is absent from Cadart's team of engravers, and it is almost certain that his prints, which he exhibited very seldom and which were only known to a few close friends like Rouart, Lerolle, Bracquemond, and Mary Cassatt, exer-cised but little influence. At the sales which took place after his death was revealed the first part of a work consisting almost entirely of portraits. Degas, who belongs to the same generation as Manet, produced his first plate in 1856, at the age of twenty-one. It is his *Torso*. Apart from the *Pressigny* by Ingres, there were as yet very few portraits among the etchings of the XIXth century. The finely crossed hatchings on this plate, as it appeared in its original state, show that Degas was still saturated with classical traditions : he frequented the Cabinet des Estampes as assiduously as the Louvre. The subsequent stages through which the plate developed bear witness to a spirit not easily satisfied, a spirit which, having started by a close analysis of reality, ends by expressing itself in simplicity and nobility. Right from this first attempt, we feel ourselves in the presence not only of an admirable draughtsman («I am born to draw», as he himself said), but of a *born engraver* who looked upon the etching as a means of expression with its own laws proper to itself. The first stage of his portrait is light in tone and little bitten. A succession of further attacks with the acid, followed by the dry-point and an erasure here and there with the burnisher infuse new life and power into the background, and the aspect of the plate is so modified as to produce an effect of chiaroscuro.

Degas' biographers do not tell us who it was who initiated him in the art. Was it the engraver Tourny whose portrait he executed in Rome in the following year? His real master was Rembrandt, whose works he had copied (the picture of the young man seated, deep in thought), and whose influence can be seen in the small portrait of M. de Gas, the artist's father. Several other etchings show remarkable precision in an impassioned rendering of character and individual expression. They may be described as traditional in the noblest sense of the word, having no age and seeking no outward pictorial effect.

As Degas was copying the *Infanta* of Velasquez at the Louvre, straight on to the plate without any preliminary drawing, he was approached by Manet, who exclaimed : " What, have you the audacity to engrave in this manner? That is a thing I would not dare to do. " We have very little information on the links which were later to unite the two artists, who never ceased to exercise an influence on one another. Bracquemond advised them both. The year 1864 is marked by the three half-length *Portraits of Manet*, drawn seated and carrying a top-hat or with his hands crossed. In the first of these plates Degas had recourse to grain, a practice often followed by Manet himself. The evolution of Degas's style is shown in these portraits by the familiarity of attitude, the surprise effect of a peculiar movement, and by a freer arrangement of the figures. The charming *Marguerite Degas* (1865) could be regarded as a reversal to a more classical conception if it were not for the movement of the muff in the foreground, an artifice of style which reappears in many of Degas' later prints.

The importance of this group of portraits could hardly be overrated. After a silent lapse of ten years Degas added another plate to this collection, and entitled it *Au Louvre*. The upright format is important not only for the originality of composition, but also for the methods of working on it which can be followed through twenty different stages. The general design, the perspective, and even the distribution of light and shade are modified by the introduction of successive grains, by new cuts and erasures, a constant interplay of precision and simplification. It is a work which reveals to its full extent that tension and thirst for perfection which are characteristic of Degas, who was not afraid to exclaim : " There is no art which is less spontaneous than mine. "

While Manet hardly ever introduced any modifications into his etchings, Degas was, apart from Pissarro, the only artist of that generation whose scruples and whose perpetual desire to improve on the original conception can be followed in the many stages through which his plates developed.

12

Towards 1875 appeared the first of the *Danseuses*, treated in a combination of point and light grain. The erasures of the burnisher here play the same part as the scraper does in lithography. There is an increase of extremely complex methods of working, which produce great variety in the disposition of black and white, and even in the very aspect of the plate and its wrinkled surface : furrows hollowed out by the acid, rough edges left by the dry-point, vibrations produced by the roller, half-tones produced by soft varnish, and the grain-work of aquatint in the midst of which empty spaces stand out (lamp-shades of the music hall, dresses dazzling under the bright lights, flames of gas or lamp light on the ironing women's table or on the bodies of the models). " For Degas " wrote Paul Lafond " engraving was both a source of amusement and a means of expressing his thought, and not merely a method of transposing his work from one medium to another. He has recourse to every recipe, formula, and trick which have been known or used to a greater or lesser degree, and sometimes long abandoned. He employs every instrument which is pointed out to him. He uses the soft varnish which for three-quarters of a century has been held in such disregard, varnish for repeated corrosion, flour of brimstone, glass paper, brush, grains, and dry-point, barbed and not barbed. He works away at his plates without break or respite, giving them ever more precision, making one attempt after another, biting and biting them again. Paper and inking, too, concern him no less. "

Paul Lafond was right in using the word " trick ". Degas' skilful tricks, however, should not in any way lessen our admiration for his talent, for they are entirely in the service of his inspiration, and are the manifestation of his conscience and his modesty, his desire to surmount the greatest difficulties. Never does he hanker after pictorial or, outward effects; in his work richness of theme is always inseparable from the high standard of draughtsmanship of which we can follow the evolution in his engravings with unabated interest. As his technical skill develops, his treatment becomes synthetic, he seeks to grasp the form in movement, and from a long maintained silence he breaks out into expression. The clever early portraits are left far behind. Not that Degas is now more easily satisfied, for the number of stages in his engravings is constantly on the increase. There were, as we have seen, twenty in the case of Mary Cassatt at the Louvre, eight in the *Dancers in the Wings*, thirteen in the *Bath*. Paul Jamot, at a time when it was fashionable to pick Degas to pieces, said that he had " launched the ideas and invented the subjects which his friends later turned to their own profit. " And what he wrote about Degas' canvases we can apply equally well to his engravings : " Degas has been privileged to handle subjects which hitherto had only been attempted by genre painters. The beauty of his work is revealed under an aspect as strange as it is precious, in the manner in which he has transformed the genre engraving by endowing it with a force as noble and with a groundwork as rich and complex as are to be found in the finest creations of the great writers of romance.

MANET AS ETCHER

Although Manet, like Corot, looked upon the process of engraving as a matter of secondary importance and left it to friends and printers to do the biting and produce the impressions, although he seems never to have taken the trouble to become thoroughly versed in the technique of the art, even his slightest attempt on copper reveals such power and such decision that the professionals themselves have been forced to admire this layman who knew everything by instinct and who, like so many great writers, has not had the time to acquire greater accuracy.

As in the case of Courbet, Manet's mind only worked when the paint-brush was in his hand; the greatest of his compositions was only sketched in rough outline, and his draft design rarely presented a complete embryo of the finished work. Engraving was for him a side-show, but it was superb. True greatness in an artist is revealed in every aspect of his work, and a study of Manet's etchings and lithographs gives a clearer insight into his character, a better judgment of his evolution, and a more accurate measure of his immense influence.

Manet appears to have had little encouragement in his work as an engraver, even from his admirers. His first album of five etchings appeared in 1862, but Baudelaire made only incidental references to it, and this lack of appreciation continued for a long time.

The catalogue of his works which was published in 1906 showed that the number of plates which never saw the light of day during the artist's life-time was almost equal to the number of plates published. The existence of many of them was only revealed when the collections of Bracquemond, Burty, Degas, and Guérard became open to inspection. Like Corot, Manet had no close ties with the printers, and he left it to his friends to bite his plates and draw the impressions. Engraving for its own sake had little interest for him; it appealed to him more as a means of multiplying his drawings. The fine points of its technique left him unmoved. It is even surprising to find that from his early years he made attempts in the complicated process of aquatint. Had it not been for Goya, would he have ever set his mind to it at all? The whole process must have appeared to him as a simplification, as an easy method of achieving contrast and colouring.

At the age of twenty he engraved *The Gypsies* after a painting which he later destroyed. Here we already find him, as in the first album of etchings which was published in 1862, not drawing his inspiration direct from a model, but rather acting as a very free interpreter of his own canvases (*The Guitar Player*, *The Absinthe Drinker*, *The Street Boy*, *L'Espada*, *The Little Girl*, etc.) or of the masterpieces of the Spanish School (*The Little Cavaliers*, *Philip II*, etc.) This explains the somewhat slow tempo and the atmosphere of *pose* which lay the imprint of the studio on some of his engravings, in strong contrast with the deep-rooted impetuosity which becomes apparent in his design when he draws with greater freedom, with spontaneity and not after a previous composition.

Would we be justified in including Manet, as Léon Rosenthal has done, among the " dynamic " masters, such as Rembrandt, Rubens, Delacroix, Daumier, and Degas? He has neither their memory nor their sense of movement. His figures, though very much alive, are almost invariably represented seated or standing, in a static attitude. If there is a parallel between him and Goya — and the *Exotic Flower* is inded a pastiche of *Bellos Conselos* — it is due less to affinity of temperament and subject, than to the fact that Manet served his engraver's apprenticeship in *Les Caprices*. He follows the same system of small short hatchings, parallel, punctuated, and not crossed, which infuse a restless energy into the background — a system in which Goya himself was preceded by Canaletto. His stroke is vigorous, his furrow clear and bright. Rich blacks and intense whites are produced by his bold handling of the point, and the whole is permeated with delicate feeling. There is a vigour suggestive of Rembrandt in the long parallel gashes with which he has marked certain parts of " *The Toilet* ", an admirable work which recalls Chassériau. Note, too, the almost Venetian colour-play of the cloths and cushions in the second stage of his *Olympia*, contrasted with the absolute white of the body and the opaque black of the background.

Perhaps the most significant of all the plates are those which Manet engraved in the simplest manner, without recourse to aquatint and without the advice of his technically-skilled friends (Bracquemond and Guérard). To this group belong the *Ballerine*, the *Philosopher* (whose bearded face, black hat, and body draped in a cape stand out with such vigour against a streaked background full of movement), the actor *Rouvière in the part of Hamlet*, the *Child with a Sword*, and the amazing *Queue outside the Butcher's shop*. This last plate, which was discovered after the artist's death, should no more be considered a finished work than any of the sketches in the manner of Eva Gonzales or Berthe Morisot. Nevertheless, even in its unfinished state, it shows that Manet should not only be looked upon as a " traditional master of the first order " — to use an expression of Gustave Geffroy — but as a true forerunner. Here the forms are merely suggested by a system of small parallel hatchings, and the masses appear in parts to be consumed by the light. In common with the Impressionists, Manet was the first to anticipate in his engravings — far more revolutionary in this respect than those of Whistler, Degas, or Pissarro — that *complete disintegration of forms by light* which eventually led to the *suppression of contour*.

It is never safe, of course, to generalise from plates left in the sketch stage. A number of his other etchings and lithographs, however, as we shall later have occasion to observe, bear witness to a more and more pronounced desire, doubtless influenced by the Japanese works of Degas, to present no longer, as in the early works, a static attitude or the " legal form " (if we may be permitted to use such an expression, applicable as it is to the question under discussion), but the unexpected aspect of appearances divorced from their natural element and disjointed by every manner of conflict.

THE LANDSCAPE ENGRAVINGS OF COROT, JONGKIND, DAUBIGNY, AND THÉODORE ROUSSEAU

It is as a spontaneous genius who appears in all innocence to be ignorant of the rules of the game and bares his flank to the enemy's criticism that Corot makes his first appearance as an engraver. His technique is wholly instinctive. Temperament, however, can always work miracles. Corot appears never to have gone through all the stages of biting a plate; he never made a single drawing straight on to the stone. He is one of those whom M. Coppier, the learned author of the analysis of Rembrandt's " handwriting ", would have classed as an " engraver pressed for time ". The fact is that Corot, like Jongkind, never attached any great importance to this particular aspect of his work, and when he did set his hand to drawing on copper, glass, or transfer, it was only by way of amusement or to oblige a friend. It was Bracquemond who, long after it had been engraved, did the biting of Corot's earliest copper, the *Souvenir of Toscane*, which had been discovered at the bottom of a box of nails. In spite of the uncertain conditions in which this plate was executed, it shows great decision of stroke and an inborn ability to place the values in their true position. Corot's prints should be studied in conjunction with his drawings. The earliest, which are traced with blacklead fine and sharp as steel, come as an introduction to his etchings. We can see that the others are of the same period as glass plates and autographies by the vivid stripes of the charcoal and by the way in which the mass and the general colour scheme are brought out while detail is eliminated. The glass-plate, however bastard a process it may be in itself, was for Corot an excellent preliminary training for the etching. He practiced his hand on about fifty heliographs before producing the *Souvenir of Italy* (1866), the

Surroundings of Rome, the *Italian Landscape*, the *Wooded Landscape*, or the *Dome of Florence*. His lithographs, too, published in 1872 in the *Album de Douze Croquis*, profited by the experience which he had gained in etching.

Although many of these engravings were produced far from the scenery which inspired them, their emotional force has not diminished. " In my heart and in my eyes I preserve a copy of every one of my works, " said Corot. A study in oils inspires him to make an etching, a drawing begets a glass-plate, and the spirit of nature is recaptured in both the parent and the offspring. While working in his studio he still hears the voice of the springs, of the winds, a great harmony of voices. No technical difficulty can dull his communion with the *rediscovered* landscape. After an interval of several years, the theme loses none of its power. The very title of " souvenir " which he is so fond of giving to his prints (*Souvenir d'Italie, Souvenir de Sologne, Souvenir des Fortifications de Douai*) bears witness to this amazing fidelity. Looked at from close, these prints give the impression of a confused scrawl. By moving back from them, however, one becomes aware of a strict order which governs their tangled lines. Every form, every shape is described by Corot in the one and only way which truly corresponds to its character and its movement. Every stroke, however little stressed, has its meaning. A slight touch with point or pencil here and there adds a little shade to a fold in the soil, to an outstretched branch, or sets off the pure white of a birch, a tower, or the sky. The restrained scale of values is maintained in the whole plate, and every note rings true, clear and precise like the chiming of a bell.

The " photographic etchings " to use Delacroix's expression — of Millet, Rousseau, Charles Jacques, Daubigny, and above all Corot — deserve a renewed interest on the part of the artists and the public of to-day, now that photography itself, after years of discredit and sterility, is at last becoming an art. The impressions, made for the most part on stiff paper, have preserved all their freshness. Some have acquired that faint coating of verdantique so that they resemble old drawings yellowed by centuries. The *Petit* and the *Grand Cavaliers sous bois*, the *Souvenir d'Ostie*, and the *Gardens of Horace* are not in any way inferior to the best etchings and the best autographies. The figures are sharply cut and almost sparkle, a word which we may surely use in describing the gentle strength of the point applied to the coating of ink or collodion. Often, too, the light of day, as though reflected in a crystal prism, gives a scintillating play to the print and endows it with an added magic charm. It is as though the original drawing had been sharpened and strengthened.

**

The work of Jongkind, together with that of Géricault, Delacroix, Daumier and Rodin, ranks among the most original productions of the XIXth century. It consists however of only twenty-two plates spread over a period of sixteen years (1862-1878). The ease with which this artist expressed himself, from the very first efforts collected in his *Cahier d'Eaux-fortes* (1862), shows that he would have been ready to trace on copper the thousands of subjects which his alert sensibility and power of observation collected during his bohemian wanderings.

The majority of his etchings are descriptive studies of Belgium and Holland; another group recalls his fondness for the Norman coast where, under a sky with its mobility and grace reminding him of the sky of his native land, he rediscovered Boudin, Cals, and Courbet. A third, more limited group is inspired by the streets of Paris. We find no trace, on the other hand, of Jongkind's travels in the Nièvre district, in the South of France, or in the Dauphiné, where he was to end his days.

16

Though by their outward appearance they may give an impression of brusqueness and rapid execution — to which certain technical experts objected — Jongkind's engravings possess a degree of certitude which could never have been the product of improvisation. As in the case of Corot, the painter's admirable visual memory allowed him to reconstruct, from a few living notes still lingering in his mind, the full scale of the emotions originally experienced.

Neither in his letters nor in his conversation did Jongkind ever make any allusions to his engravings. On one occasion only, when speaking to the critic Fourcaud about two plates which could not be found, he said : " They are only junk (sic) which belongs to the time when they wanted to make an engraver of me. I began with these trifles and did not carry on much further. " He never engraved direct from nature, and he never elaborated his subject. Sometimes the etching preceded the canvas (as in the case of the *Entry into* and the *Departure from the Port of Honfleur*), sometimes it came after it. While drawing his inspiration from his sketches, Jongkind readjusts everything quite naturally when passing from one technique to the other. He modifies not only the contours and the general layout of the landscape, but also the distribution of values, of light and shade, and the movement of the sky. The sincerity of the work is never damaged by this apparently unconscious process of synthesis. In every case it is the profound and lasting element of an impression that is conveyed in the execution.

It was not through mere fancy that Signac reproduced the *Pont de Six* in his remarkable work on the drawings and etchings of Jongkind. The very subject of Rembrandt's masterpiece differs hardly at all from the subjects which were treated a hundred times by his compatriot, a striking example being *The Moored Boat*. The affinity, however, is not merely superficial. Their kinship is of the spirit. It is in their skilful use of perspective, in the subordination of detail to the whole, and in the art of obtaining the maximum effect with the minimum number of lines that the two masters resemble one another. Rembrandt's *scrawls* — as Diderot called them — foretell those of Jongkind.

Nothing, of course, was more alien to the nature of this good Dutchman than tidiness. We know that he worked with any instrument at random, with the handle of his paint-brush as well as with the brush itself, and that often the pigeons which fluttered around his canvases added their discharge to his colours. In the same way, he took little pains with his engravings. There are plenty of cracks in the varnish, of odd spots of acid, and of strokes gone astray. He does not even take the trouble to invert his signature. When examined through a magnifying glass his lines appear bizarre, chaotic, and dishevelled; they cut across one another without any regularity. When Méryon engraved he held his point extended like a rapier. Jongkind's hand appears to tremble (and it must indeed have trembled at times under the influence of alcohol); in spite of all its apparent hesitancy, however, it is none the less obedient to orders of the most exacting character, to the slightest reactions of an exceptionally keen vision. Here, too, we find that gimlet-like, hooped, and saw-toothed design for which Rembrandt's analysts have sought a definition; and at the same time, though the two artists did not know one another, we find Daumier's angular, broken, and uneven strokes, marvellously varied in depth and intensity. That monster, the straight line, as Delacroix called it, is wholly absent here, even when it is called upon to describe the horizon : Jongkind insists on reminding us that the earth is round. No one is more naïvely arbitrary; nobody else would venture, in defiance of all scholarly canons, to underline the intensity of a value, or, in order to convery the full depth of feeling, to make contrasts vivid enough to stir the white of the sheet to life, as he does.

Not only living beings, but also objects and even the very planes, if one may say so, are endowed by Jongkind with an intensity of expression and an extra-ordinary movement. The earth and the sky take part in an action which unfolds in all its fulness as far as the horizon and which continues to the right and to the left, without our being aware of its limits. The most outstanding example is *The Sunset at Antwerp.* It is the first stage of this plate that should be seen — not that the later stages underwent any modifications, for in the majority of Jongkind's etchings the differences are merely small ones of adroitness — but the fresh copper has produced blacks which are clean and light, while in the later impressions they are smeared and dirty. In the foreground on the left there is a boat. In the second plane, a three-masted craft in profile against the sky and, not far off, another ship with spread-out sails. In the background, the coast. The sun is setting in a kind of clear mist which penetrates the foliage and cuts off the tops of the church steeples. What is amazing about this plate, an example of Impressionist art at its highest, is the skill with which the vibration of light is expressed, penetrating the forms, separating them out of the mass, and transfiguring them anew. Viewed at close quarters, it is an inextricable jumble, like a mop of fine, tangled hair. As one draws away from it, one is struck by the precision of the small cuts and of the little dots, so true in their intensity and their angle. In parts the incisive and insistent strokes have almost laid the copper bare; in other parts they have merely skimmed over the varnish. There is the water, opaque and ethereal at the same time, in which thousands of scintillating lights are mirrored, there are the concentric zones which expand around the orb of pure gold. We can almost hear the pulsation which animates the whole scene, and in which even the clouds share. It is true that the beauty of the subject has added to that of the print, which is one of the masterpieces of the XIXth century, but we find the same qualities in the views of *Maasluis*, the *Entry* into and the *Depart-ure from the Port of Honfleur*, as well as in the *Demolition of the rue St. Marcel* and the *Departure from the Hopital Cochin*. They are plates which have the feeling of winter, of the distress and weariness of the old streets, and which express, perhaps for the first time, the pathetic aspect of a disease-stricken landscape and of alleys of stone and mire over which whistles the breath of a moving sky, ablaze with colour.

***

Corot attached little importance to his engraved sketches. They are, however, together with those of Jongkind and Whistler, the most characteristic examples of the evolution of the rendering of landscape in the XIXth century. Everything is expressed, thanks to an analysis of values and an amazing vibration of line. We shall not find the same qualities again till we come to the etchings of Ségonzac.

" I am never in a hurry to get down to detail, " Corot wrote in his note-book. " Mass and quality are what interest me more than anything else in a picture. " No doubt, if he had had the time, Corot might have perfected his craftsmanship, which the practical theorists of engraving will always criticise for its summary character. It may be, too, that he would have found in lithography a better medium for conveying his message, in view of its closer analogy to pencil and charcoal. One must admit, moreover, that he was more of a stranger in engraving than, for example, Jongkind or Rousseau.

The fact remains, however, that Corot's few etchings soon exercised a pre-ponderating influence over a whole group of minor landscape artists, such as Chauvel and Appian, who, though they failed to reproduce any of the inimitable notes of Corot's voice, remained faithful to its timbre and to its favourite harmonies.

Daubigny, whose stupendous industry and creativeness never slackened throughout the period from 1838 to 1877, served them as model to an even greater extent, and that in spite of his avowed cult of Ruysdael and Claude Lorrain, in spite of the sincerity of his response to the phenomena of nature, in spite of the strong element of lyricism which permeates the *Sunrise*, the *Spring*, and the *Tree with Crows*, in spite of that sentimentality to which he is very prone, of that silvery light of the morning or of orchards and ploughed fields in moonlight. The effect of these landscapes is often weakened by a certain timidity, by an abuse of contrasts and an overloaded style. It is precisely this same tendency to excessive minuteness and overapplication that led many an engraver astray in the period between 1865 and 1880.

The number of engravings that have come down to us from Théodore Rousseau and Jean François Millet is very limited, and the influence which they exercised appears to have been considerably less far-reaching than that of Daubigny and Charles Jacques.

Théodore Rousseau, one of whose rare masterpieces in engraving, the *Oaks at Roche*, appeared in 1861, showed all the signs of being an admirable engraver, with more method in the arrangement of his cuts than Corot. His first etchings, his heliographs (*The Cherry Tree*, *The Plain of the Plant at Biau*), and his vigorous studies in pen drawing only make us regret that he was little more than a stranger in the field of engraving.

MILLET, LEGROS, RIBOT, RODOLPHE BRESDIN

The influence of Millet does not appear to have been any greater. Living in seclusion at Barbizon, where he found the solitude, the plain, the forest, and those immensities of land and sky which seem to have been essential to his happiness, he added little to the first sketches which he etched mostly about 1885 with the advice of Charles Jacques, with the exception of the *Chicken-Feed*, the *Sheep-fold*, the *Setting out for Work*, and *The Spinner from Auvergne*. These masterpieces of his prime are cut with a strong, vigorous hand. Silhouettes of powerful men and women fill almost the whole of the plate, their heavy clogs planted firmly in the soil and their faces hardened by the fresh air and the inexorable trend of the seasons. The admirer of Mantegna, Pieter Brueghel the Elder and Van Ostadt, here deliberately turns his back on the gentle grace of the XVIIIth century. Whether he is treating figures or landscape, he emphasizes the principal planes and the main folds, and he presents everything under an aspect of eternity. The forms are ennobled by a kind of natural solemnity; familiar objects draw their lifeblood from a calm seriousness; they are well-balanced, and the carding woman and the shepherdess tend to become statues without any effort. In his sculptural qualities, in the poweful, clear-cut simplicity of his principal lines, and in his skilful elimination of all secondary detail Millet comes very close to Daumier. His faith — faith in man and faith in nature — hallows the meanest of his engraved sketches and gives them a solemn message. In his design he finds himself quite naturally speaking in the language of the prophets. None of the accusations which have been brought against this art, especially that of attaining style by sheer artifice, can be maintained in front of these great plates which contain a whole life's experience expressed without complacency or emphasis, but with a kind of solemn stoicism.

Millet, like Méryon, widened the range of his art by the practical experience which he gained in etching.

For all their qualities, the masterpieces of Millet were never destined to reach the great public. There was one man, however, whose genius was kindled by their grandeur and who acquired from contact with them an originality which, unrecognised in France, found refuge on the other side of the Channel. Though not a peasant's son like Millet, Alphonse Legros lived close to the soil and from his childhood days breathed the air of poverty. He never forgot the rustic cadences and the rites which seemed to attend the labours and the humble meals of the countryside as well as the religious services. Nurtured in the great examples of the past and fortified by that visual memory which he developed under the influence of Lecoq and Boisbaudran, Legros, like Millet whom he greatly admired and whose style he closely approached in his deep, wellspaced hatchings and his seriousness, drew broadly and slowly. While it was the drama of labour and resignation, however, that formed the subject of Millet's art, the romanticism of Legros expressed itself in more violent scenes where man is shown at grips with his destiny and with all manner of cataclysms. Death, which to Delacroix only appeared through the medium of Shakespeare and to Millet through the medium of some of La Fontaine's fables, never ceased to haunt this visionary. Though falling short of Daumier, whose quest of style was more unconscious, or Rembrandt, in whose prints we find sullen distress hovering over the faces and the hands of his heroes and over some of his landscapes, Legros never stooped to the petty pictorial effect and the facile pathos which after him were cultivated by many a virtuoso in etching and dry-point, who supplemented " literary " effects with the artifices of the engraver's craft and faithfully exploited the art of misery. His greatness is quite independent of any anecdotal or descriptive aids. The lessons which he taught his pupils were boldness, promptness in attack, and rapidity in execution : those very same qualities, in fact, to which his own engravings — the pale, light-coloured prints cut with thin, slender lines as well as the vigorous designs with the dramatic accents sharply underlined — owe their peculiar beauty. He was a master in the art of biting; no other artist watched that most important stage of the process of etching with greater attention. Simple and accurate in his orchestration, he knew how to distinguish melody from accompaniment, how to effect a contrast between the paleness of the background and the rich vigour of the outline, between the muffled vibrations of the dry-point and the clear-cut resonance of the etching. Every figure and every landscape which he created moves us particularly by the simplicity of the means which he employed. This erudite artist, who was filled with a passion for the individuality of character, produced some engravings which, together with those of Ingres and Gaillard, may be regarded as the finest masterpieces of the XIXth century (*Cardinal Manning, Dalou, Edwin Edwards, Poetic Ecstasy, The Spanish Beggar*). That mixture of passion and reflection, which is characteristic of Legros and relates him to the Primitives, attains the greatest success in his portraits. Compared with them the portraits by Bracquemond seem to be cold, those of Desboutins superficial, and those of Zorn boisterous. However charming or profound are the drawings which he cut with gold or silver point, it was on copper that the innate engraver's instinct of Legros really surpassed itself. France is still unaware of the importance of this silent master who flourished over fifty years ago, and the number of whose works exceeds eight hundred.

Théodule Ribot, influenced both by Rembrandt and the Spanish school, deserves to be recalled from the oblivion to which lovers of art have consigned him, if only for the sake of his small studies of interiors, his figures, and his still-lifes which are remarkable for their virility and frankness. Knitting-needle, kitchen knife, and the point of the burin were all used with equal freedom by this artist in his engravings. The acid, which often ate through the coat of varnish, has added to the power of a stroke which shows no hesitation in attacking the metal and uses wide rings or majestic hatchings, occasionally coloured by a grain of aquatint. The most natural and unartificial effects of chiaroscuro enable Ribot to concentrate all the light on the faces and hands of his figures.

*
* *

The work of Charles Méryon does not come within the scope of our study. His series of *Eaux-fortes sur Paris* was executed between 1852 and 1854. By 1862, with the exception of the *Bain froid de Chevrier* and the *Ministère de la Marine*, almost all his important engravings had appeared without meeting any success. His spirit was distraught by persecution mania, hallucinations and poverty; he filled his compositions with flying human figures and birds of prey. Even in his madness, however, there was a certain lucidity : his goal was clearly visible to him, and he was not astonished when his methods of expression appeared " bizarre and somewhat risky ". He emphasised that the objects portrayed in his plates were " beyond positive representation ". The time was yet to come when critics were to agree with Baudelaire that " in the severity, the fineness, and the certainty of his design, Méryon recalls that which was best in the etchers of antiquity, " and that " one has seldom seen the natural solemnity of a great capital represented with more poetic feeling. " The engravings of Méryon, which enjoyed an exceptional success, were soon to reap a prodigious fortune, especially in Anglo-Saxon countries. Artists began to imitate his metallic strokes which turned stone into bronze, and his deeply-bitten furrows, and they lost themselves in his architectural details. Then, instead of this passionate analysis and devotion to detail, they acquired a precision of line and a strength which however was lacking in sincerity. A minute, punctillious realism was fettered to the natural gifts of the visionary, and countless " city landscapes, " coloured by the printer's artifices devoid of the essential elements, parodied the art of Méryon, like the thousands of stilted country landscapes and thread-bare forest scenes which were but feeble copies of the art of Corot.

*
* *

Contemporary with Méryon, another great *solitaire*, whose life was no less strange than his character, brought out into the light of day all the hidden treasures of the art of black and white. This man was Rodolphe Bresdin.

There are very few documents which throw light on his artistic origins and education, and the contradictory evidence of writers, largely led astray by his eccentric personality, only tends to make the legend that has been woven around him still more obscure. His first attempts at engraving are dated 1839, when he was a youth of seventeen. Several of them are little larger than a postage stamp. If the current story is to be believed, Chien-Caillou printed these etchings with the aid of blacking and a boot-brush, and sold them to junk dealers at a few francs apiece. In 1848, at Toulouse, where he executed a lithograph of *The Good Samaritan*, he lodged in a kind of cattle-shed peopled with birds, cats, and rabbits. In his sad moments he ended his letters : " Your friend in spite of the rain and the wind. " In 1869 he was in Paris. His eyesight grew weaker, and he was given up for lost. He had disappeared without a trace for a long time when one fine day in 1876 he was seen entering a café, loaded with luggage and followed by a wife, six children, and a negro. He had realised the dream of his life, which was to settle down in America, but, once there, he only met with disappointments. Later, having been appointed Assistant Gate-Keeper of the Arc de l'Etoile, he lived in the heart of Paris, in an attic which, to the horror of his fellow-lodgers, he turned into an orchard spouting streams of water. In 1885, having no other source of income than the fruit of his little garden which he marketed at a low price, he died from congestion of the lungs at Sèvres in the large bed of white wood which he had made himself.

These picturesque details help us to understand his work. Whatever contacts Bresdin may have had with Paris, he appears to have remained quite untouched by anything in modern art. He continued to live and to think in a world apart, or rather in *worlds* apart. The novels of Fenimore Cooper, in which he had discovered a surname for himself, gave him the illusion of being a free man and a savage. His huts strewn with stubble and peopled with birds, his gardens which he never cultivated, his rabbits, his green frogs, and his spiders are the clues of his art.

Bresdin was never tired of repeating that " a true artist need never even look at nature. " This is indeed a strange remark coming from a man whose patience bordered on folly, and who delighted in picking out, one by one, the countless roof-tops of a distant town, the blades of grass in the field, the branches of a forest, the cracks of a cliff, the ripples of water and of the clouds. Incapable of drawing from a model, he took refuge in a precarious shelter of the mind where his imagination ran riot and fashioned an artificial world peopled with marching legions, tribes in flight, hermits and Holy Families, and all the beasts of creation. He had visions of forests of lances, of peoples swarming like vermin, of veiled and turbaned women, cenobites, unicorns, thousands of steeples and minarets piercing the sky.

Part of his work has a freakishness which recalls Hieronymus Bosch, Brueghel the Droll and the devilries of Callot. Bresdin, however, to attain his effects of mystery, needs neither the baroque nor the macabre. It is from the most familiar forms, from the interplay of light and shade, and from all the incomprehensible elements hidden behind common appearances that his art derives its beauty and its *grandeur*. Bresdin gives one the impression of having surveyed the world through a magnifying-glass, and it is with magnifying-glass in hand that one should scan his teeming landscapes in order to wrench from them their countless secrets. In other artists' work such minuteness would have been exasperating. Bresdin, however, is diametrically opposed to the odious race of miniature painters, and it is in the service of the infinite that he takes such pains to be finite. Never, when elaborating his microcosms, does he lose the feeling of the whole. We have only to look at his masterpieces : *The Good Samaritan*, the *Holy Families*, the continuation of the *Revue Fantaisiste*, the *Peacocks*, the *Comedy of Death*. A world restless with activity palpitates and is transformed under our gaze; there are extraordinary analogies between the several domains; in spite of the profusion of detail, there are no sections which are dead.

Bresdin's technique never varies, whether he engraves on copper or on stone. Myriads of tiny points, far finer than the finest grain of aquatint, cover the whole plate. This niello-work is so delicate that one can well understand that the artist ruined his eyesight. *The Calvary of Gros Caillou* was continued. To the very end, *he carried his stone.* At the age of sixty he found consolation in the same hallucinations, and his last etching, in which all his favourite subjects are reassembled — masts, steeples, palaces, thatched cottages, barges, roaring waters, and wind-torn clouds — is entitled : *My Dream.*

CLAUDE GAILLARD AS ENGRAVER

For a long time both critics and lovers of art looked upon the plate cut with a burin as being the only respectable form of the art of engraving, while the etching, and especially the lithograph, were regarded as something second-rate. Up to the end of the last century — as we can see by the sales of prints — the majority of the big collectors took little interest in anything but the feats of technical virtuosos who took it upon themselves to interpret the masterpieces of other artists without showing any signs of personal talent, nor even the reflected talent of genuine interpretation. If we look through the plates worked under the spell of Ingres, we might think they were all cut by the same hand. There is the same icy-cold composition in which every trace of the true style is obliterated and which seems conceived for the special purpose of rendering a Meissonnier or a Roybet without any risk of going astray.

In 1868 a Society for the encouragement of interpretative engraving was founded under the auspices of the *Gazette des Beaux-Arts*. At its head was Henriquel Dupont, who was a suitable leader, for he had distinguished himself as an innovator at the Ecole des Beaux-Art, where he taught copper-plate engraving and brought about a sort of revolution in the art by combining the point with the burin and varying the arrangement of the strokes, thereby avoiding the monotony of regular lines. He had himself engraved several fine portraits. His prestige delayed the decline of a technique which received its death blow when the process of photographic reproduction was invented. The *Société des Graveurs au burin* made unavailing efforts to safeguard the interests of its members and, by a succession of exhibitions, to give a fresh lease of life to their out-of-date craft on which vast sums of money were expended. Five to ten thousand francs were the prices paid for some of the plates — a very considerable sum at that time. Eugene Delacroix had already denounced in his Journal the errors of those who " sought brilliant effects after their own fashion by training their hand to a style which was only capable of clouding the impression. " " The engraver's language, " he said, " does not only consist of imitating the effects of painting, whose language is quite different. " The engraver has a language of his own which, while giving a faithful rendering of the work it imitates, allows its own particular sentiment to find expression. This is what Bracquemond was never tired of repeating to his brother craftsmen. He struggled against the spirit in which the classes of engraving were conducted, and he deplored the oppressive uniformity of engravers who cultivated the technique of cutting to the detriment of everything else. " One study class, one engraver, " he exclaimed : " the Institute. " And again, later : " In the prints of the old engravers who worked under the guidance of masters of painting, the surface of the paper is never completely covered, for in an engraving, paper gives the effect of light. With the engravers of the school it is quite different : they are so preoccupied with cutting that they allow their design to spread everywhere in great profusion. A Rubens engraved by them has the same colouring as a picture by some minor painter devoid of originality and life. "

Out of the nameless brood whose dreary, stereotyped lozenges covered the monotonous copper-plates for so many years, one artist alone found favour in the eyes of Bracquemond, because he was a great designer : Claude Gaillard.

This Franciscan lost in the modern world was indeed a marvellous figure. Without having the originality of Ingres, Delacroix, or Degas, he was impelled by the same passion of delving deep into the laws of art in general. Whether it was the *Joconda*, the *Man with a Carnation*, or the *Pilgrims of Emmaus* that he worked on, he discovered a new message in these pictures and enriched them with his own blood at the cost of thousands of proofs and endless toil. We can see how, in his preparatory sketches, he analysed in turn the whole and the details, particular spots or contours, or how he sought the aid of sculpture or of a living model in his efforts to understand a picture, to become the complete master of those great paintings of the past, with the result that his burin not only faithfully rendered their external aspect but conveyed the very essence of their soul. In his complete self-effacement through love of the work of former periods this priest of the third order had no equal among his contemporaries, and approached the spirit of the early masters. With regard to him it may indeed be said that the art of the burin wished to be sunk and to die in beauty. In every one of Gaillard's plates there is so much passion in his search for the equivalent of colour, such genuine respect for every value which he seeks to convey in a new medium, that even in his engravings which were but reproductions of other artists' work, he may with justice be considered as an original engraver.

On several occasions — but they were far too rare — this master who had never belied either Van Eyck, Donatello, Raphael, or Rembrandt, resumed the fulness of his own individuality and, in a technique which has the true modesty of erudition, revealed a man of his own period who yet belonged to every period, who sought and found the eternal essence in the transient, no matter whether his subject was a pope, a king, a count, or a soldier. The portraits of Dom Gueranger, of Sister Rosalie, of Pius IX, and of Leo XIII are some of the most moving which have ever been engraved. Their beauty is derived from a depth and a firmness of sentiment which lend an added inspiration to the craftsmanship. One is even tempted to say that these portraits move us in spite of their complex and laboured composition, to which the artist is bound as though it were some discipline imposed upon him, almost a mortification of the flesh. So great is the volume of labour accumulated in each of these works, some of which go through as many as thirty stages, that one feels inclined to ask how, in an age when etching was becoming more popular largely owing to the rapidity with which it could be executed, an artist could wish to continue engraving with thousands of little points and tiny, close cuts, and by what miracle this craftsmanship, as minute as a goldsmith's, was carried to completion without the spirit ever being sacrificed to the letter, without the execution ever stifling the sentiment, without detail ever trespassing on the whole. Here indeed, as Beraldi put it, " the engraved line is a means and not an end. "

We, with our restless temperament, must make a real effort if we do not wish to be unjust to this art, or to be put off at first sight by some of these plates, to which the framework inspired by XVIIth century borders gives an antiquated appearance. A superficial critic will fail to grasp at once the accents, the contrasts, and the short cuts of Gaillard; he will not perceive the inner fire of inspiration : hence he will condemn him as a sluggish and faint-hearted spirit. The truth is, however, that this excess of thought and scruples does not cool a passion which is constantly controlling itself. Let us take the first versions of *Dom Gueranger* or of *Sister Rosalie* : here the plate, bitten by the acid, has the " look of skin pitted by smallpox "; or, to put it differently, of old wood eaten by worms. There can be nothing less systematic than the methods he employs : burin, scraper, burnisher, hammer, and dry point are brought in one after the other. In the successive impressions we can follow the engraver's hesitations, his violent strokes, his contradictions, his alterations. At times he starts off from a stage in which the mask is modelled as though by a sculptor, with a few bold strokes he brings out character and introduces the imprints and ravages of age; then, with this as a basis, he works up towards expression, softens the contrasts, and gives the humblest of faces a look of the divine. At other times he begins with an analysis of over-developed detail, eliminating later what

24

is unnecessary; he called this the drop of water method. At other times again, he drew in first the main decisive features; then, owing to his profound knowledge of all the processes of engraving, he was able to blend them together in the elaborate design of the same plate. In this way, as Roger Marx has claimed, " he achieved results unknown to any of his predecessors. "

For all the significance of the lesson taught by Gaillard and the profit which artists such as Waltner or Patricot derived from it, in spite of the official patronage given to the burin by the Institute, that instrument of which Félix Buhot had foretold the end in *L'Illustration Nouvelle*, was no more to be used by great artists, with the exception of the Belgian Peter Dupont, until the days of the great engravers of the XXth century : Laboureur, Soulas, Hecht, and Decaris.

II. – THE REVIVAL OF LITHOGRAPHY
ABOUT 1862

CADART'S INITIATIVE — DAUMIER'S LAST LITHOGRAPHS

At the same time as he was busy establishing the *Society of Etchers*, Cadart had three stone plates sent to Bracquemond, three to Manet, three to Ribot, three to Legros, and three to Fantin. " Together they were to make an album, " Hediart explained. " Manet produced the *Balloon*, Ribot, the *Reading Lesson*, Legros the *Quarry-Men of Montrouge*, and Bracquemond *The Riders*. Fantin, who was handling a lithographic pencil for the first time in his life, showed himself to be the most eager of them all, and used all his three stones. When they were returned to Lemercier there was an outcry. They were branded as detestable, insane, wild, and unfit for publication. "

The reception with which Fantin's *The Embroideresses* met at the printers differed little from the one given to the first attempts of his companions. Only very few impressions were made. Cadart was compelled to abandon his plans of publication, with the result that the revival of lithography was delayed for over ten years.

Lithography had blossomed too quickly; its vitality had been sapped, and a long period ensued during which artists and editors found in it little more than an economical means of reproduction. Delacroix was content to let Mouilleton or Le Roux interpret his works on stone. Bertaut ceased publishing the *Artistes Contemporains*, which had included the lithographs of Doré, Nanteuil, Français, and Baron. Printers used the process for little else than title-pages for popular songs. " All that is left, " wrote Burty, " is to bury the last pencil-holder under the last stone, and to engrave upon it the words of the vanquished patriot : finis lithographiae. "

Vicomte Delaborde wrote in the same vein in his review of the Exhibition of 1878 : " Lithography, as understood and practised to-day, has lost that spontaneity which was its principal charm. It is becoming a simple process of reproduction, and has almost forfeited its *raison d'être*. " The indifference of connoisseurs to original lithographs was even greater than their indifference to the etching. And yet week after week, in the *Charivari*, Daumier continued to publish masterpieces.

Many writers have remarked that Daumier, disgusted at having to " pull his own cart, " as he himself put it, bridled by censorship, tired of having to draw inspiration from his bourgeois surroundings and from the grotesque reality of daily life, had allowed himself to run to seed, and that during the Second Empire his engravings lost all their vitality and became mere repetitions of old subjects. The truth is that until the last volumes of the catalogue illustrated by Loys Delteil were published, his work was very little known. The *Souvenirs d'Artistes* were the last of his lithographs which the *Charivari* published " on white, " as it had done in the case of the *Men of Law*, the *Good Bourgeois*, the *Robert-Macaire*, the *Ancient History*, *What you wish*, *The Bathers*, *The Blue-Stockings*, and many other admirable series which we shall not dwell upon here as they are so well known and have been popularised by many reproductions. On the other hand, the voluminous tomes of the *Charivari* during its decline would find little praise even from the most fanatical admirers of Daumier. The poor quality of ink and paper, the slipshod printing, the substitution of " gillotage " for stone — all these defects tend to falsify the magnificent orchestrations of black and white which preserve their splendour only in the very rare first proofs.

Betrayed by the public and by the publishers, Daumier was never a traitor to himself. He had, of course, his periods of weariness, especially about 1865, when he reverted (in the *Journal Amusant* and the *Journal pour rire*) to the system of enormous heads on top of miniature bodies. Apart from this, however, his design, far from weakening, became more and more full-blooded. The oblivion to which the public consigned him, gave him more leisure to paint, and the many lithographs which he executed almost concurrently with his canvases are more full of colour than ever. The epic genius of the designer awoke within him. Muzzled as far as home politics were concerned, Daumier devoted a large number of plates to the European conflicts of the time. He drew more and more on the fund of his imagination, and substituted great symbolic figures for real characters, typical examples of that period of his work being the *Last Council of the ex-Ministers* and the *Parricide*. No other artist of the XIXth century had a greater command of allegory. Ruthless in his attacks on sham antiquity, he had a keener sense of the grandeur of past ages than any of his contemporaries (I quote Baudelaire). The same tunics which draped the actors who burlesqued the *Characters of the Classical Tragedy* were henceforth used to clothe the pathetic and moving figures of *France* and *Peace*. Statues semi-nude under their garments were modelled with one spontaneous effort of his hand. Antiquity not only supplied him with the costumes, it also lent him its deities, as *Time*, with scythe in hand, accompanies *Death*, and *Mars* hastens on, *Europe* barely maintains herself on a smoking cannon-ball. *The Future* is clad in a wrestler's loin-cloth, with bandaged eyes and a scythe and sand-glass lying on the ground. The *Savings Bank* : every nation prepares its pile of cannon-balls. The *Statues of the Future* ? Polycarp the Gunner, Eustace the Marksman, and Barnabas the Machine-Gunner. *Progress* — a blindfolded horse turning in circles. *Not too short* ? Liberty asks the Constitution, who is trying on a new garment. The year 1869 is shown rolling an enormous Budget, like Sisyphus rolling his stone. War breaks out. Death, leaning against Bismarck, points to a plain strewn with corpses. *The Empire is Peace* ? — nothing but smoking ruins. *Square Napoléon* ? — nothing but gravestones. A landscape in 1870 : a cannon in the midst of ruins. The Empire falls : *Punishments* has crushed the eagle.

For the third time Daumier seized the whip-cord of political satire. The suspension of the *Charivari* prevented him from taking part in the struggle between the Versaillais and the Communists. France is presented as a tree with a blasted trunk; " *Fortunately*, " reads the caption which can be applied equally well to Daumier himself, " *the roots are firmly planted*". His *Peace* (an Idyll) is Death wearing a shepherd's cap and sounding a trumpet, seated on a rock. *She is risen at last* : France, propped on Loan, raises herself erect to the astonishment of the whole world. One of his last lithographs, *The Witnesses*, may be compared with the best plates which he had published in the reign of Louis-Philippe; here we see a whole crowd of skeletons — one beheaded, another leading a child, and another pointing to the Council of War — all shouting for vengeance and moving towards the court room where Bazaine is facing his trial.

Whether he did or did not invent his own captions during this period, Daumier illustrated them with the same impulsive ardour that had animated his earlier work.

27

Michelet's prophesy came true : *You alone have the stamina, and it is through you that the people shall find voice to speak to the people.*

Apart from their captions, and even apart from their subjects, in spite of the treacherous handling which they suffered from the printers, these lithographs are unrivalled. The generosity of the plastic means employed in their production is coupled with the generosity of the artist's heart. Daumier's philosophic visionis widened, and his imagination soars on a higher plane. There is nothing small either in craftsmanship or in sentiment; we always find the same common sense, the same candour proof against all trials, the same smile bred of power, experience, and resignation. The four thousand plates of the *Caricature* and the *Charivari* will provide future ages with the clue by which they will discover the true spirit of XIXth century France. Their topical value will never fade and their allusions to events which if Daumier were not the artist who treated them, would now be lost in oblivion or devoid of interest, remain true for all time and have such a powerfull appeal that every generation can find in them comments upon the events of its own period.

MANET — COROT — FANTIN-LATOUR

" It was the lack of a public, and not the lack of artists, " wrote Burty, " that was responsible for the death of engraving. " At a time, however, when lithography appeared to be given up for lost, when officially it was looked upon as practically non-existent, a number of individual ventures which sprang up on all sides proved that the art was still very much alive.

Though fewer in number than his etchings, the lithographs of Manet are an even better guide to his power of feeling and to the quality of his design. We can trace in them an influence of which rhe extent has not yet been sufficiently recognised, that of Daumier. Hard to discern in the *Balloon*, which was his first effort on stone, it becomes more clearly apparent in *The Barricade*, and especially in the *Civil War* (1871). Even apart from the analogy which may be drawn between the tragic room of the *Rue Transnonain* and Manet's corpse of an insurgent lying with its back on the ground, we are struck by many a resemblance, due to a common technique even more than to similarity of subject; we admire in the plate the accents in the design, the firmness of composition and the mastery of style. Then again, in *The Race*, with the three horses galloping abreast towards us at full speed, the sense of movement is communicated to the whole plate and we have the feeling that the stands, the railings, and the sky are carried away by it just as much as the horses. The men and women who form the crowd can hardly be discerned; they have lost all individuality and are nothing but dark patches. It would be difficult to find another plate where rhythm reaches such a pitch of acceleration.

Manet's contribution to portrait engraving is not less marked. His two studies of *Berthe Morisot* — the one treated in contour alone, and the other emphasizing the face framed by the hair — have that incisive style and forestall that tendency of abbreviation which was later to be both used and abused by the artists of the XXth century. The influence of Japan shows itself in his illustrations for the *Raven*, where, thanks to that colouring peculiar to lithography, Manet rediscovers the blacks of Edgar Poe, and in the *River* of Cros (1874) for which he designs this time on copper, a series of landscapes full of a spontaneous charm truly revolutionary for that period. The *Polichinelle*, which belongs to the same year (1874) is in itself less significant, if only for the fact that it comes as a prelude to the revival of coloured lithography which, twenty years later, was to be vindicated by Lautrec and the painters of family scenes brought up in the studio of Clot.

28

We have already mentioned the album of twelve autographies which Corot designed at Arras and Douai in 1871, in which all his power of feeling remains unimpaired, so much so that even his use of transfer, which with other artists would have tended to produce a blurred uniformity, here helps to bring out their etherial quality. Following the advice of Th. Way, who was responsible for the revival of lithography in England, Whistler engraved his first nocturne, circa 1878. About 1875 Degas began to try his hand on the stone, showing the way (in *Au Cirque Medrano*, the *Song in the Café Concert*, and *Mlle Becat*) to Toulouse-Lautrec. No doubt, too, Forain would never have developed as he did if Degas had not engraved the *Nude woman at the door of her room, Behind the scene in the theatre* or the *Nude women at their toilet*. His influence can be detected here not only in the choice of subject, as with Lautrec, but in the actual design. Degas' lithographs go through fewer stages than his etchings. The *Box in the front of the theatre*, as also the *Song of the Dog* and *Behind the Scene in the theatre* appear to have been drawn at one sitting. On the other hand, *The Bath* and *The Nude woman at her toilet* (engraved about 1890) while they reveal a manner more abrupt, contours more and more summary, and a disdain for the laboured craftsmanship of his earlier works, betray at the same time that passionate urge for self-correction which in his old age caused Degas to go over many of his canvases and pastels again and again, and sometimes to spoil them. The roller and the scraper have been used so freely in *After the Bath* that in its second stage the work is barely recognisable.

We shall see later that Pissarro, too, in a series of twelve studies of family life, contributed to an art to which Rodolphe Bresdin was to remain faithful. The most important contribution of all, however — not so much in its intrinsic value as by its quantity and by the spell which it exercised over artists who were at first reluctant to start upon the stone — was without a doubt that of Fantin-Latour.

The art of Fantin gives one the impression of being mainly concerned with transposition : herein lie both its charm and its limitations. Even when his compositions are taken straight from life and not from the caprice of his dreams, they still bear the stamp of the Museum and the Theatre. He is often inspired by his own pictures. The *Bouquet of Roses* (1879), one of his masterpieces, and the *Eve* were modelled on his canvases. This is a method which tends to put a brake on inspiration, a defect which is still further accentuated by the blurred effect which the use of transfer produces. " After he had finished tracing his design " — so Hediard tells us — "he left it as it was, barely making any of the essential retouchings which are necessary in order to add finish to the print. " Here we come up against one of the most serious problems of the art of lithography. While the use of transfer relieves the artist of all cumbersome manipulations with the stone, its danger is that it makes him forget all those aspects which can only be truly brought out by preserving direct contact with the stone plate. Lithography by transfer soon ceases to be an independent art with its own proper technique, and in its monotony becomes little more than a convenient method of reproduction. The only legitimate use of transfer is to lay down the first outlines of the design. It is essential, however, that after this is done the lithographer should come back to the stone and touch it up with wash or pencil, adding more shade where it is required and making the necessary alterations with the scraper. It was not long before this was understood by Odilon Redon who, after he had learned the use of transfer from Fantin, made a practice of collaborating far more closely with the printers. As a result his technique became superior both to Fantin's and to that of a number of other artists, such as Renoir, who had recourse to autograph paper.

Fantin's lofty spirit, his culture, and the subtle understanding with which he endeavoured to reconcile the real with the imaginary give an exquisite charm to his work. Nevertheless he lacked several of the virile qualities. Though at times he came very close to the spirit of Lamartine, he did not possess the style of the latter, and he did not redeem his effeminacy by those epitomes so common in the work or the author of the *Meditations*. There is always a certain hesitation and uncertainty about his work. Everything takes place in a silvery, misty world peopled with chaste figures living in mid-air between heaven and earth, half-way between life and the theatre. The setting in which they move is reminiscent of the *chiaroscuros* of Corot. Fantin had good taste, a gentle charm, and a sense of that beauty which is the offspring of order, but he lacked a sense of life. Even though he was the favourite pupil of Lecoq de Boisbaudran, he had none of that visual certainty which gave Daumier and Degas their power. He worked from memory, but his memory was weak. His best engravings, too, are perhaps those in which he forced himself to give a faithful rendering of a bunch of flowers, his own face or those of his sisters reading or embroidering, in the calm light of an interior. Here we find a concentrated tenderness of sentiment which sustains the force of the design. The profound idealism of his studies in pencil or brush has the effect of moving us both by his scruples concerning the outside world and by the suavity of the atmosphère in which are bathed both living beings and familiar objects.

Many of the lithographs to which Champfleury applied the term " Schumanistic " owe their titles to the symphonic poems of Berlioz, Brahms, Schumann and Wagner. They come as an echo, somewhat dull and sad, of the Venetian splendour. It was from Titian, Veronese and Giorgione that Fantin appears to have taken his Eve and his Venus, and one cannot help being moved by the quality of an art which succeeded in deriving so much charm from the art of black and white. When we turn over the leaves of this work which contains over a hundred and fifty prints, we can imagine what a lithograph by Seurat would have been like. There is often the same art of creating zones of glittering light by contrasts and of making the white of the paper flash like lightning through contact with the black. In the case of Seurat, however, as in the case of Redon the mysterious element outweighs the anecdotal aspect : the most ordinary forms and people who have nothing legendary about them are presented on a higher plane. It matters little that more than once carried away by the force of his own invention, or excited by the contagious influence of the masters whom he paraphrased, Fantin let the narrow framework of his dreams crack under the strain. There were moments when he closely approached the masters of the XVIIIth century and Prudhon. No other painter — with the exception of Daumier, but in quite a different way — was able to make allegory as alive as Fantin did, or to pay due homage to painters, musicians, and poets, to inspire the breath of life into the pearly figures of women carrying palms and garlands, or again, by engraving their names on white flagstones, to invoke the images of Glory, of the Muses, or of Liberty, without relapsing into coldness or emphasis. For he whom Anatole France described as " the painter of friendship " possessed a perfectly natural nobility and greatness of character.

THE LITHOGRAPHY OF ODILON REDON

While the influence of Bresdin can be clearly detected in the first attempts on copper which Redon executed before 1870, his first series of prints, " The Dream, " (1879) shows that by that date he had acquired an independent personality. Up to the year 1900 concurrently with his paintings, his plates followed one after the other, revealing one of France's greatest designers since the time of Delacroix. Redon would no doubt never have become the master that he was if he had not beheld the ceiling of the *Apollon* or *Jacob's struggle with the Angel*. However, the emotion, which we experience when we look at the *Captured Pegasus*, the *Centaur aiming at the Clouds*, the *Reader*, the *Closed Eyes*, or such admirables series as the *Dreams* and the *Temptations of St. Anthony*, is quite different from the one which Delacroix inspires in us. Redon's prints are full of allusions to the Great Unknown which surrounds us, to those aspects of things which cannot be explained and to the proportions which our existence would assume if it were guided by a different star.

Some of his compositions, it must be admited, are not only striking but irritating in their strangeness ; they are gruesome fantasies or burlesques full of wandering eyeballs, larvae with human heads, and giggling monsters. This part of his work, which was the delight of J. K. Huysmans and which gives rise to every manner of misunderstanding, appears in our judgment to be out of date. We admire Redon's imaginative genius when, restraining his feverish licentiousness, he contents himself with his true aim — that of *going beyond the object*, of freeing himself from the bondage of the real, of breaking through the ceiling (*the ceiling of the Impressionists is too low for me*, he once said). It is then that we admire him without reserve, just as we admire Dürer, Hieronymus Bosch, Brueghel, Leonardo da Vinci, Callot, Tintoretto, Goya, Delacroix, or Bresdin, who had trodden the same path before him, and whose plastic hypotheses, far from appearing childish and derisive, conquer further fields in the art of painting.

Redon, observing what Rémy de Gourmont called the *logic of imagination*, took care never to wound our reason. He twisted the subject without losing touch with reality, and often had recourse — to use his own term — to that *abstract line* which his apprenticeship in architecture and his study of shadow projection had enabled him to analyse. Without being a slave to the traditional optical canons, he distributed his light centres at will. The most important element in his work was the composition of light, to which was subordinated the subject matter or the setting of the subject. There were few artists who could blend the most diverse values with such strength, or distribute so skilfully the sources of warmth and life. At times his blacks and whites clash with a tragic violence; at other times darkness is slowly and gradually penetrated by the light. The whites, according to whether they are enclosed in pitch dark night or surrounded by soft shadows which are toned down by contact with them shine with the brilliance of gold and bronze, flash like the ether or preserve the passivity of stone or the sadness of snow under a dull sky. Here the light, brilliant greys have the gentleness of rippled water, the fine grain of a transparent skin; elsewhere we see them drawn out in streaks of heavy mist or falling in a compact network. And then again, there are the blacks : abysmal blacks as abstract as the Idea of Death itself, and velvety sumptuous blacks, brilliant as purple, blinding as the sun. Seurat alone, perhaps, in his use of " conté " pencils, reaches such heights of splendour. These works, which are technical masterpieces quite apart from the subjects treated, and which delight our eyes before they delight our spirit, could be compared with those summer skies that strike wonder in us not only by the allusions which they contain to that which is inaccessible and cannot be explained, but also by the contrast of glittering patches of light with deadly gulfs of darkness. Such is the magnificence of these designs on stone, that we do not even stop to think of that effort of abstraction whereby the artist has succeeded in suggesting everything merely by the skilful manipulation of lines and values. Colour, which as such is employed in only one or two prints, is none the less suggested in all his work.

After tracing the main contours with the aid of a transfer, Redon toiled over his stone as assiduously as Delacroix, whose scraper brought out all the clear values of his admirable *Macbeth consulting the Witches*. In order to oppose glittering whites to intense blacks (often reinforced with wash), he used glass paper, and he frequently furrowed the granite so deep that several milimetres had to be pumiced. These irregular methods were a source of annoyance to the professionals. Redon has given us an account of the hours which he spent with the printers in the press (and they were excellent printers, such as Belfond of Lemercier's press, and Clot), and of his work on the fine stone of Munich, impressionable as a woman, capricious and moody, mistrustful or yielding without reserve. " I believe, " he wrote, " that I have given full play to my imagination, and left it to its own devices, in the hope of finding all that lithography could give. All my plates are but the fruits of an eager analysis of what could be obtained with the thick pencil of a lithographer, aided by paper and stone. "

At other times, without having recourse to the magic of chiaroscuro and without using wash or scraper, he designed in simple contours. This was the technique employed in his engraved portraits, scattered over the period between 1900 and 1908, which represents the concluding stage of his work as a lithographer. Nowhere else can we observe so well his faithful observation of reality as in these portraits of friends, which are executed with the precision, the penetration of vision and the motion of the pencil studies of Holbein and Clouet. In fine and serried strokes the thick pencil gives precision to the bony structure of the face and its characteristic features; there is no emphasis on external beauty, no easy emotive effect by stressing a smile or a look. And yet, natural and supernatural at the same time, these portraits bear that resemblance to the sitters which at that period only Degas, Lautrec, and Carrière succeeded in expressing, and even then by quite different means. An examination of these portraits will no doubt provide food for reflection for those critics who look upon Odilon Redon as a writer who missed his vocation, while in fact he never ceased, with that clear understanding which stands out in all his writings, to " *demand yeast and leaven from nature,* " to " *endow the most unreal creatures with an illusion of life* " and to " *place the logic of the visible at the service of the invisible* ".

III. - THE ISOLATION OF PAINTER ENGRAVERS FROM 1875 TO 1890

FELICIEN ROPS — TISSOT — DESBOUTINS

Now that we have completed up to the end of the last century our analysis of the work of a number of engravers, masters of a profoundly individual art who were appreciated only by a limited circle of connoisseurs, we can return to a group of artists who enjoyed a wider popularity with the public at large.

We have already mentioned that Cadart carried on his efforts after 1880 in the *Illustration Nouvelle* and the *Eau-forte Moderne*. The *Gazette des Beaux-Arts* and *Art* (founded in 1875) provided an opening for a certain number of engravers, while *L'Artiste*, rich in the laurels of a splendid past, was making its farewell appearance with Rodin's *Victor Hugo*. In the meantime, interpretative engraving continued to monopolise the attention of both dealers and amateurs. In 1878 the following prices were recorded in Cadart's catalogues : Manet, proof of the *Gypsies*, six francs; collection of ten proofs of Jongkind's etchings, sixty francs; an album of six etchings by Delacroix, thirty francs. Fifteen francs was the price asked for a proof of Méryon's or of Seymour Haden's. This state of affairs lasted almost up to the end of the century, and in any case up to 1889, when the *Society of French Painters-Engravers* was founded. As we turn over the publications of the societies who set out to defend professional interests, we find very little space devoted to original engraving. The Society of French Lithographers, the Society of French Etchers, the Society of Engravers with the Burin — none of these showed much intuition in this respect, any more than the international exhibitions of the Art of Black and White. Nothing could have been less complete than the retrospective exhibition of engraving organised in 1892, from which the works of Géricault, Delacroix, and Manet were entirely absent. The Exhibition of Lithography, organised in 1890 by Jean Gigoux and Français, and that of the Centenary of Lithography, (1895) alone appear to have been exemplary displays which sought to establish a connection between the present and the past.

At that time, moreover, etching, which was only reproduction, tended to supplant the burin. Engravers such as Gaucherel, Jacquemart, Chauvel, Waltner, and Focillon toiled scrupulously at the interpretation of other artists' work. Laleuze, Champollion, and Le Rat produced in great number their small book illustrations and vignettes. The public was fascinated by Meissonnier, and the etching was soon to suffer from a surfeit of detail and from the coldness which had been the death of the burin. It was a triumph of the gloomy, laboured engraving, deprived of all imagination and plastic intelligence. On this bleak background stands out in solitary prominence the work of Félicien Rops.

For a period of nearly thirty years he eclipsed all his fellow artists. The smallest book adorned by one of his frontispieces fetched a high price. He rallied the votes of the experts as well as those of the great public. In his first lithographs published in the *Charivari*, which were done in the style of composition design, everything appears to be borrowed from Daumier or Gavarni. The originality of the etchings is not of the highest order; the design is faltering, and the craftsmanship lacks freedom. Never could the term soft-ground etching be better applied. Just as in his water-colours this ingenious master had recourse to processes of illumination and to every kind of complication so also in his engravings he successively availed himself of every imaginable process. In all his work, however, his hankering for literary and theatrical effect got the better of pure fantasy, and virtuosity prevailed over good craftsmanship. Rops was one of the first engravers to have recourse to a background of heliogravure. It was a dangerous example. A background produced by a mechanical process of photography took away from the original character of the print from the very sart.

There were many critics who imagined that in the *Absinthe Drinker*, *Messaline*, *Dancing Death* or *Mors syphilitica* poetic values found their true interpretation in plastic art, and who were ready to believe, for the sake of naturalism and symbolism, that this gipsy was a brother of Baudelaire and Edgar Poe. To-day *Robbery and Prostitution dominating the World*, the *Aged Faun*, or the *Woman with a Pig* appear childishly erotic. In spite of the profusion of tiny Cupids, the fantasy displayed in the vignettes is far from winged. Morin and Willette, direct descendants of the charming masters of ornament of the XVIIIth century, were inspired in quite another manner; they excelled in multiplying the emblems, and in combining the ingenuity of the printer with the profusion of their themes. Whatever admiration Rops may have had for the Parisian woman — " that incredible mixture of pasteboard, nerves, and rice powder, " to use a phrase which he coined — his attitude towards her was always that of a provincial in search of adventure or of a dumbfounded student. We need not believe Ramino when he describes this off-hand design, which constantly degenerates into effeteness and doubtful artifice, as possessing " an integrity equal to that of Ingres. " It is only through those plates full of the rich tang of the soil — *Old Catherine*, *Flemish foolishness* or the *Old Chisel* — where his powers of observation and genuine feeling have been given free play, that the work of Rops can claim to survive. The rest of his work reminds us only too often of the old garters, ribbons, and other intimate objects that one discovers with horror in the wardrobes of the dead.

We are no less astonished at the fame which James Tissot enjoyed. Although he possessed a ready appreciation of elegance, this was but the privilege of an artist whose work owes its renown to fashion and is as fleeting as fashion. Yet a day comes when these works are rediscovered and enjoyed as witnesses to a past period. The same will doubtless happen to the drypoints of Paul Helleu, which, after enjoying too great a renown, were put on one side.

Desboutins said of the etching that it was " the horror in the poultice. " This was a way of expressing the mistrust he felt of the risks that so often attend the process of biting. We would have been inclined to agree with him, had it not been for the fact that he himself, crippled by work which he had to carry out to order and which dulled his inspiration, fell into the ways of facile artifice. His most successful efforts are his dry points executed at one sitting, which, drawn with vigour and natural good sense, are excellent resemblances and full of life, particularly the small portraits of several of the best artists and writers of his time, and that series of portraits in which, under such titles as *The Man with the Pipe*, *The Man with the Palette*, and *The Man in a big Hat*, he represented himself without burdening the plate with too many strokes.

Rops, Tissot, Desboutins, Helleu, and many other minor illustrators enjoyed a considerable period of renown as master engravers during the last years of that XIXth century which was so resolutely hostile to any form of originality and which had so little attention to spare for the treasures that lay fallow in the portfolios of Degas, Pissarro, Rodin or Carrière.

THE WORK OF BUHOT, ZORN, AND BESNARD

The position of Felix Buhot (1847-1898) is difficult to define. A romantic at heart in the heyday of realism, moulded in the school of Hervier — a charming chronicler, ofter a visionary, of the life in small ports —Buhot soon abandoned picturesque anecdote and began to execute plates inspired by his travels in England (his two Westminster plates and the *Landing*), by his long sojourns at Valonnes or by his visions of Paris (*La Taverne du Bagne, Place Pigalle*, and others). Daubigny loved the morning, Buhot preferred sadness and mist. He is at his best in his studies of twilight creeping over great cities and the sea-shore. No other engraver could express so well the night atmosphere of London or Paris, the noise of wet pavements, the slippery gait of passers-by armed with umbrellas, like strange birds sailing between heaven and earth. It was with quite a different feeling that Méryon, Whistler, and Jongkind had described the great capitals.

No artist, with the exception of Degas, made use of such a complex craftsmanship; he impetuously combined every imaginable process in his concoctions, varying the shade of the ink and the quality of the paper, and adding one or two retouchings to his proofs by hand. For this subtle complexity of process he invented a charming name : he called it the *little chamber symphony*. He surrounded his plates with a framework of little remarks and variations on the central theme, and he called these his *symphonic margins*.

The Little Pond, The Big Cottages and *The Sheep Fold* are depicted with a familiarity full of noble feeling. His lyrical power is revealed in the great symbolic pictures, such as *The Spirit of Dead Towns* and the *Castle of the Owls*, as well as in those designs on essence paper and those etchings which suggest the effects which Victor Hugo might have obtained from copper. Buhot's whole life was, as he himself put it, nothing but a " succession of proofs. " A victim of his own ink, he became engulfed in mysticism and in darkness. " My proofs, " he wrote, " have entirely devoured me — both my time and my brain. " A curious figure, whom one could place beside Chien Caillou " bearing his stone, " and beside all those for whom the art of engraving was more than a craft, it was an obsession.

It was during the time that he spent in London (1879-1883), where he made the acquaintance of Legros, that Albert Besnard was initiated in the qualities of copper. The emotional force of *The End of Everything*, though undoubtedly strong, is dominated by a kind of decorative splendour in which the actual composition and the vibration of light are equally manifest. It has been said that it was Rome that made Besnard. Would it not be truer to say that it was Venice ? There is a distinctly Venetian opulence about the *Portrait of Madame Besnard* and the *Silk Dress* (1877). Using his favourite effect of counterlight he succeeds, with remarkable ease and quickness of spirit, in achieving true harmony between his vigorous cuts and his slight incisions, the barbs of his point mingling their silky blacks with the more candid blacks of the acid, and thereby creating voluptuous contrasts and passages, and a symphony of mirrored lights. Besnard's work varies greatly from one print to another, but his qualities of grace and lustre, emphasised by the candour of his biting, are just as pronounced in his *Dans les cendres* as in *The Ill Mother* or in *Reading by Lamplight*. This lyrical artist knew how to make use of the conquests of Impressionism. He had the feeling of the open air *(The Bathe at Tallories, The Horse Market at Algiers)*. Great streaky hatchings in the style of Degas appear on a number of his plates. His portraits, in their brillancy, anticipate many of the qualities of Zorn. He was a virtuoso who often allowed himself to be carried away by effect and by a superficial lyricism, but who nevertheless found copper to be the best medium for his talent. The renown of Besnard the engraver was to be far greater than that of Besnard the painter.

*_**

One of the signs by which a born engraver may be recognised is that unexpected inspiration which he receives as soon as he touches copper, wood, or stone. Many artists who would otherwise never have left the groove of modest repute accomplished feats in engraving which neither their temperament nor their intelligence would have allowed us to foresee. I am thinking particularly of Anders Zorn, whom we beg to claim among the French engravers, as it was amongst us that he had his first success. It was not till 1884 that his own individual hand became fully developed. Form is defined by small parallel engraved lines of amazing swiftness and vivacity. One might say that the style often resembles that of Manet, but it is still more feverish. The light is caught between the lines and the movement of planes is suggested by distribution, as in sculpture. Accelerating the tempo of his stroke till it becomes quick as lightning, Zorn easily executes fifty portraits with great rapidity. There is in this somewhat electric art an abrupt charm which compels admiration. The metal, as though surprised by the impulse of a point firm and yielding at the same time, sings in response to the caress. One can understand the enthusiasm aroused, at a time when Impressionism was becoming fashionable, by the portait of *Rosita Mauri*, where the same line is continued like a lasso, hardly marking the border-line between the form and its own shadow where it streaks the plate like a sulphur match and creates a charming face in a light which one could hardly describe as artificial or natural. In spite of the apparent brilliancy, however, of the *Portrait of Ernest Renan, The Cigarette, The Waltz* or *the Toast* — all masterpieces of a kind in sincerity of movement and expression — these works belong to an art which in the long run comes up against limitations. In spite of his gift of instantaneousness, Zorn was never destined to reach the depths which Legros or Rodin fathomed. His nudes, however dazzling, have often a trivial touch. Even in the presence of a lady of fashion from London or Paris he does not drop his habits of a peasant. This healthy straightforward sensuality has its charm. But if he had turned to *Verlaine* or *Renan* for an answer, Zorn would have detected only one small aspect of the truth. His work is summary rather than synthetic. Of sadness he is ignorant. His dazzling gleams of light are never accompanied by the tragic resonances of drama which we find in the works of great artists. Zorn never felt the urge to fathom the depths that lie behind a face. Though often compared to Rembrandt, he is more akin to Van Dyck ; and he displays in engraving something of that direct force which Courbet introduced in painting.

THE DRY POINTS OF RODIN

The work of Rodin, though limited to eleven prints, is the most important contribution which any sculptor has made to engraving. It was in 1881 that Rodin, who was then living in London with Legros, tried his hand on copper for the first time. *Love leading the World* dances on the reverse of a plate engraved by Legros. The

Spring and the *Round Song* are dated 1883. " In the portraits of *Victor Hugo, Becque,* and *Antonin Proust*," wrote Roger Marx, " which were executed between 1884 and 1886 — and I would here bow before him who first emphasised the importance of these engravings — Rodin achieved the full expression of his ideal. He uses a burin slightly tapered like a chisel or a rasp, and handles the copper as roughly as he would handle his Carrara marble; the violence with which he attacks the metal, however, gives way to caresses as soon as the main outlines are supplemented by a cross design of close lines. These lines mark every inflexion of the model for they follow the direction of the relief of the forms. In the engravings which emerge from this contrast and accumulation of strokes, we can perceive the artist's struggle with his matter and follow the stages by which the peculiarities of the surface are revealed. They are works unique in their vitality and in the astonishing variety of their relief, portraits which suggest the mould of a sculptured bust, bring out the details of flat surfaces, and play in glossy reflections on the polished surface of marble. "

Rodin's animated portraits are as masterful as those of Dürer, Rembrandt, Ingres, and Goya. Even the works of Manet and Degas have a chilly air when placed by the side of these works which look as though they had been called out of lightning, while those of Zorn and Besnard no longer shine, except in agitation. Let us look at the *Victor Hugo in full face* : by a marvellous insight the face of the poet is made the meeting-place of night and day; his pupils open like abysses in which the whole world is about to be engulfed; nevertheless there is no excess of emphasis in this portrait. The attitude is severe, we might think that we were looking at a little notary on whom the mantle of genius had suddenly descended.

The Round Song and *The Spring* are contemporary with the Indian ink and gouache designs inspired by Dante's *Inferno* in which the dynamic force equals that of Michael Angelo, Rembrandt, and Daumier. By his analysis of *plane* alone, sustained by a superb sensuality, this man of humble origin rises to the level of men of genius and of the most subtle masters of analysis.

THE ETCHINGS OF PISSARRO, SISLEY, AND MARY CASSATT.

Of all the Impressionists — taking the word in its widest meaning — Pissarro appears, together with Degas, to have made the most important contribution to engraving, from the point of view alike of quantity and quality. Monet always refused to touch a graver or a lithographer's pencil. Cézanne, Renoir, Gauguin, Sisley and Guillaumin only turned at intervals to lithography or etching. Pissarro, on the contrary, with his characteristic lucidity and tenacity, and with that supple, bold intelligence which enabled him to submit to very diverse influences, acquired the mastery of a complex craftsmanship which he constantly enriched by his labours.

He spoke little of his etchings, doubtless because at that time engraving was little appreciated by his friends. Nevertheless, it was his lifelong passion. He attached so much importance to this part of his work that he never ceased, both in his note-books and on his proofs, to keep a detailed register with the names of all his impressions. We know cases when the same etching went through nine, ten or even sixteen stages. And when we say stages, we are not using the word in the rather childish sense in which it is often used by collectors; we mean a series of successive *works*, in which not only the outward action, the lighting and the atmosphere of the engraving are modified, but also the composition. Conscientious, anxious to capture the essence of emotion by going beyond the sensation experienced, he often breaks away from reality in order to express it all the better, bringing in a new character in one place and suppressing one in another, reinforcing a foreground, softening a background, correcting an attitude. Masterly in his expression of the seasons, he clothes a bare tree with its foliage, lightens or darkens a sky, arranging according to his whim rain and twilight, and altering the distribution of shadows. As we contemplate these successive labours on the same plate we can see it coming to life under our eyes and striving through countless alterations towards unity and perfection.

In his first etchings we can clearly detect the influences of Corot and particularly of Millet. Already in 1874 he etched a masterly portrait of Cézanne. From 1879 onwards the aquatint made it possible for him to colour his compositions, to vary the values and to get the same variety of grays on copper as on canvas. Hundreds of contrasts and alterations are effected by showers of small pricks. Little, too, has as yet been said of the affinities of the aquatint with the processes of the Divisionists, whose discovery and application must have made a vivid impression on Pissarro's mind.

In the majority of his etchings he began by laying down the main contours of the design with acid or dry point. Then comes the aquatint of the grain of salt variety which was also practised by Degas. After that, a series of labours: polishing, scraping, correcting, cuts and counter-cuts. Shades and contours are sometimes reinforced — particularly by the peculiar use of glass paper — and sometimes softened. Occasionally a second grain of a different strength is added to the first, as, for instance, in the *Bather with the Geese*, in which we can follow the course of the artist's hand and watch its hesitations. When he comes to the tenth stage (and there are sixteen in all) Pissarro blots out almost the whole of his design, hammers the copper, and returns to the blonde transparency of the earlier stages. What is really admirable about this plate is that the technical skill of the artist is used to produce, not outward effect, but general harmony and emotion.

Pissarro did not work in a regular fashion; sometimes he went from the simple to the complex, but he often reversed the process in his quest for perfection. True wealth, as he well knew, is above all measured by sacrifice. Plates such as *Landscape at the Hermitage, Twilight, Women emptying a Wheelbarrow, Meadow and Windmill at Osny, View of Pontoise, The Church of Osny, Potato Harvest, The Castle of the Goose-Girl, The Church and the Farm at Eragny, Bather with the Geese, The Haymakers of Eragny* may be considered masterpieces. Pissarro's success would have been still more complete if, for reasons of economy, he had not been compelled to use zinc instead of copper; zinc possesses its own particular warmth, but soon loses its receptivity.

*

Of the artists who exhibited in the Impressionist groups, Renoir, Sisley, Guillaumin, Mary Cassatt and Berthe Morisot were the only ones besides Degas and Pissarro whose contribution to engraving on copper was of any value.

Sisley has only bequeathed us a series of four small landscapes, inspired by the riverside of the Loing (1890); they suffice, however, to render all his nervous vigour and the refinement of his vision. The more numerous etchings of Guillaumin have that same brilliancy characteristic of his canvases. Cézanne's designs on copper are limited to one small portrait and a torso. Renoir's etchings and lithographs were all executed after 1890.

Mary Cassatt, who was on friendly terms with Pissarro and Desboutins, won by her friendship with Degas the privilege to see his jealously guarded works which only became known to the public after his death. From her very first attempts, before 1880, she showed her virile qualities and the disdain for facile pleasantness which even in her graceful subjects, protect her from that softness which is so frequent a failing with masters of dry point.

Her entire work, devoted to the representation of woman and the child, is a kind of revenge for repressed maternity : unmarried, she was destined to depict the gestures of love and protection. Degas once said, looking at one of her canvases : " Oh, yes, this is the Child Jesus with his nurse. " These words sum up all the somewhat artificial element in these little scenes, where other people's children are represented, pretty, clean, smiling, and looking as though they do not know the meaning of tears. Mary Cassatt shed over these intimate scenes a uniform light of happiness without being able to enrich them with that personal experience on which Renoir, Suzanne Valadon, and Carrière drew when they depicted their own children. She was guided, however, by a right instinct. Where others often fell into ways of insipidness or foolishness, she maintained her dignity. Even when faced with smiles she never lost her sense of reason, and her care for good design always prevailed. " I cannot admit that a woman can draw so well, " Degas used to say. In all justice to Cassatt, however, it should be said that, even if she succumbed to the fascination of the xylographers of the Far East to the point of transposing their harmonies into her *Series of ten coloured engravings* published in 1891 (one of which is even entitled : " *Attempted Imitation of a Japanese Print* "), she owes very little to Degas.

Her pale plates, of which the surface is little covered, without any great contrasts of values and without additions, give the impression of having been done at one sitting. She engraved straight on to the plate, and her execution had to be rapid, owing to the mobility of her models. Her point furrowed the metal lightly, but with mastery. All that is merely accessory — the back-ground and even some of the figures — is drawn in a few bold strokes, while familiar attitudes are rendered with great charm (*The Maternal Kiss*, *The Child's Bedtime*, *The Breast* and *The Toilet*) as also are big hands holding tiny feet, and knees making a pedestal or a cradle. Equally striking are her studies of little girls and young women — *The Box at the Theatre*, *Tea-time*, *The Visit* and *The Banjo Players*. There is a curious mixture of reserved passion and sternness in this Anglo-Saxon artist, which gives a particular elegance and originality to her engravings.

The eight small dry points engraved by Berthe Morisot between 1888 and 1890, by the nature of their subjects (*The Drawing Lesson, the Girl with the Cat*) and the lightness of their technique are akin to the works of Cassatt. The sentiment is however different. The former pupil of Corot has qualities of spontaneity and tenderness which are lacking in the cruder and more rigid work of her elder colleague; a youthful spirit, animal-like in its directness, smiles through these prints; they have the guileless look of a child.. They recall neither Manet nor Renoir; Berthe Morisot is a forerunner of Bonnard.

IV. – THE ORIGINAL PRINT FROM 1889 TO 1914

THE FOUNDATION OF THE SOCIETY OF PAINTER ENGRAVERS IN 1889

After the failure of the *Society of Etchers* with the general public, a number of admirable artists worked in seclusion for twenty years, engraving only for their own personal satisfaction. About 1888 a coalition was formed with the object of uniting forces ; at the head of it were Bracquemond, who had lost none of his enthusiasm or conviction, and the charming and skilful Henri Guéraud

— two consummate masters of technique who well knew that technique without talent is worthless.

It would be impossible to overestimate the part played for fifty years by this society of idealists, of which the motto might well have been *fidelity and disinterestedness*, and which has never ceased to bear witness, in both annual and retrospective exhibitions, to the fact that there is no break between the present and the past, and that Death is only a word, for the same forces appear to come to life again under different names.

The French Painter-Engravers can pride themselves on having assembled, *without exception*, all the great artists who have asserted themselves or were discovered during the past fifty years. Here is a list of their presidents : Bracquemond, Rodin, Eugène Carrière, Forain, Besnard, Lepère, Jacques Beltrand. A glance at their catalogues shows that as soon as one master passes away, his place is filled by another; when a young artist of real talent develops, he is asked to join the group. Their generosity and foresight are exceptional. Most of the artistic salons shone with their lights from the outset of their career. In spite of differences of temperament, they form one body. After a time these differences became accentuated. The group appears to have exhausted its capital and consequently its vitality is spent. Without admitting the fact, it is suffering from advancing age, and, in order to defend its privileges, it has taken up an aggressive attitude.

The vitality of French engraving is demonstrated by the founding of this society of *Painter-Engravers*, which began at once to play a leading part in restoring confidence to lovers of art, and above all, to the artists themselves; it replaced other societies whose energy was failing and gave new life to the engravings shown in exhibitions. Ardour was rekindled on all sides. Critics, publishers, printers and dealers all pooled their efforts, although, unfortunately, they were not always supported by the general public. Soon, on the initiative of Lepère and Tony Beltrand, *L'Image* appeared as a champion for the revival of the wood-cut. In *L'Estampe Originale*, produced by Roger Marx in collaboration with Marty, were published mary masterpieces signed by Rodin, Renoir, Gauguin, Lautrec and Redon and the works of Bonnard and Vuillard were anticipated. In Vollard's albums of the *Painter-Engravers* were published works by many of the same authors, as also in *L'Epreuve*, *Pan*, and *Germinal*. So favourable was the atmosphere created that not only masters who had forsaken the print, such as Pissarro and Degas, went back to engraving, but also new recruits tried their skill at wood-cutting, etching, and lithography, both veterans such as Renoir and Cézanne, and the artists of the generation that followed Impressionism — Gauguin, Carrière, Lautrec, Maillol, Bonnard and Vuillard. Publishers whose books had for half a century been marred by the mediocrity of professional illustrators now realised that their only hope lay in collaboration with the Painter-Engravers, and soon there appeared the *Natural History*, *Daphnis and Chloe*, *Parallel*, *the Garden of Torture* and *Backwards*. Twenty years had to pass, however, before they were appreciated at their true value.

There is someting heroic about these battles waged on all sides for the print in different forms : the print in black and white or in colour, the poster and the book. There was a feeling of youthful energy in the air which, although it was believed at the time to be revolutionary, was yet closely bound to the best traditions which had so long been compromised by sterile practice, tedium, mechanical execution and all forms of routine work. It would be impossible to enumerate all those who responded to the call of Guérard and Bracquemond; we can only dwell on the great names. There had never been a time when talent flourished more lavishly, when hopes were keener, or when a greater number of artists was inspired. Unfortunately this enthusiasm and these illusions were only to last for some twelve years, and general indifference was yet again to get the better of true originality. With a few exceptions, the art of engraving from the beginning of the XXth century up to the end of the Great War lived on its past and gained no additional force.

SOME MASTERS OF THE ART OF COPPER-ENGRAVING: LEPERE, LEGRAND, HELLEU. A LANDSCAPE SCHOOL

Even more than in engraving on copper which, as we have just seen, was continually being enriched by efforts which were never destined to reach the public even though they were those of artists of so high a standing as Degas, Pissarro, and Mary Cassatt, it was in wood and stone that a true renaissance arose about 1890. However, etching and dry point still tempted many artists, several of whom, such as Auguste Lepère, Louis Legrand, and Helleu executed a great part of their work in this medium. Without discontinuing his wood-cuts (and we shall see how much energy, ingenuity and dexterity he used in this field of art) Lepère made in 1889 the discovery that etching was, as he wrote, " a flexible medium which lends itself to invention and obtains the most successful results in sketching and in the quest of chiaroscuro." Taking successively the advice of Bracquemond, Paul Renouard, Delâtre, and... Rembrandt, Lepère delighted in the surprise effects of cutting, biting and impression. After having for many years, with lens in hand, meticulously interpreted on wood the work of other artists, he felt himself at last to be an independent master, capable of modifying both the design and the composition of light. Still a vassal of Daniel Vierge, of Edmond Morin, and of his own past as an illustrator, he was attracted above all by the picturesque, which he sought in both old and new parts of the town, on the banks of the Seine, on the penny steam-boats and the omnibuses, everywhere, in fact, where anecdote is made by man. He quickly acquired a kind of mastery both in the plates devoted to Paris, *(La Bièvre and Saint Severin,* and others) and in his studies of provincial France (*Amiens, Beauvais, Reims, Provins*). While as a wood-engraver he progressed from the complex to the simple in search of a firm outline and of synthesis, as an etcher he continued to vary and enrich his craftsmanship. With that ingenuity of a craftsman which gives him so much charm, he controlled and moderated the force of his cuts and of his biting; he reinforced the effects of his plate still further by exploiting the process of printing to the full. In spite of his sincerity of hand and heart, however, and no doubt because as a young man he had to reproduce or illustrate the works of others, there was still something of the interpreter even in his most original plates. However brilliant and witty his etchings were, he found the same difficulty as Bracquemond in creating on copper masterpieces of the same standing as those he cut on hard wood. An agile hand and a well-tutored intelligence were at his command, but true originality was lacking. Prompted by anecdote more than by emotion, more impulsive than profound, his style was fashioned by technique rather than by the actual design.

**

The work of the impulsive and neurotic Louis Legrand shows traces of the erotic satanism of Félicien Rops, subsequently watered down by the influence of Degas and Lautrec. This sensual Burgundian, who won his fame by *The Carpenter's Son, A Beautiful Evening, Rosa Mystica,* and *The Book of Hours,* though sincere in his impulse, was too much of a trickster to appeal to the finer emotions. A victim of the aquatint he had, paradoxical as this may seem, nothing of the primitive about him. When he was inspired by a sincere emotion this sincerity is apparent in his work, hence the charm of some of his studies of little girls, such as the *Fleurs de lit*. Like Helleu, Louis Legrand was a victim of his own easy style, but he nevertheless helps us to recapture the characteristic features of the period.

For Renouard the etching was above all a convenient medium for recording his observations. Rassenfosse, a master of soft ground etching, is like an inferior edition of Rops. The precision and elegance of the documentary design of Lewis Brown, who specialised in military and sporting subjects, is especially evident in his coloured lithographs.

Helleu scored his first triumphs with his lucid dry points, which were drawn with the freedom of a sketch and in which the copper plate was furrowed as clearly as ice is streaked by skates. This admirer of Watteau and Lancret, whose work combined all the elusiveness of elegance with all the naturalness of coquetry, had the courage to be fond of fashion at the risk of some day appearing out of fashion. More faithful to the spirit of his time than to any particular characteristic of his model, rejoicing in setting forth the essentials even at the sacrifice of form itself, except in a few fine male portraits (*Whistler*, *Montesquiou*) Helleu never attains to anything more than a superficial grace. Whenever he tries to go deeper, he spoils everything. The more rapidly he draws, the more successful is the result. Coloured impressions, on the other hand, have deprived his design of its original qualities, lightness and distinction. The dry point cannot be reproduced indefinitely, and allows only of a limited number of clear impressions. In the case of Helleu, this number has only too frequently been exceeded, with the result that the prints to which he devoted all his nervous sincerity and his desire, when multiplied to order, betray all the signs of hasty execution and create an impression of sheer monotony and mannerism.

Side by side with Helleu we have Somm, Boutet, Gœneutte, and Jeanniot, birds of passage who defy all classifications and who specialised in what was then called *Parisian etching*. They were pleasing chroniclers. There were also Guérard, a disciple of Japan who let his mischievous fantasy have full play in his small prints, and Vignon who engraved charming little subjects. Raffaelli, a poet of abandoned suburbs, of remote tracts of land, of small crafts and small people, makes use of etching, aquatint, dry point and soft-ground etching. With great taste and ingenuity he makes his colours cover the plate as though with a coating of dust, without however dulling the charming effect achieved by the light strokes. Chahine, the bold portraitist of Anatole France and Louise France, depicted many picturesque anecdotes, although he sacrificed too much for effect. In the fairs and the circuses Brouet imagined that he found again the beggars of Callot and Rembrandt.

The great lessons taught by Corot, Whistler, and Seymour Haden have borne fruit in the French school of landscape artists up to the present day; we trace their influence in the thrill of emotion which is experienced at the sight of a stretch of water or a sky, and in the quality of a craftsmanship both modest and well-tutored. Eugène Béjot, an engraver of clear days and a serene portraitist of Paris and the ports, expressed himself in a language sincere and unencumbered, with a perfect knowledge of all that can be done by the point with or without the additional aid of acid, cutting minutely every object and every plane, controlling his emotion and leaving nothing to chance. Gustave Leheutre, as though speaking in a hushed voice, drew carefully with short, nervous strokes, which he padded with the burnisher. His etchings of provincial life, with big, empty white spaces, hardly bitten, have the appearance of dry points. J. L. Moreau was a consummate technician, master of himself and skilful in the art of biting. Jacques Beurdeley can be recognised by the silvery tone of his plates, which reflect all the delicacy and the charm of the Ile de France; like Chintreuil, he ought to be called the painter of mists and dews. Then we have Laborde, elegant and subtle; Jouas, graphic and exact; Charles Heyman, a true heir of Lepère; Collet, whose tragic romanticism found expression in etchings which look as though they had been bitten by the wind and the sea; Dauchez, faithful to his sandy moors, Eugène Delâtre, Hercher, and many others.

ENGRAVINGS ON COPPER BY RENOIR AND SUZANNE VALADON

Renoir, who never had a press of his own, only engraved occasionally, like Corot. His first soft-ground etchings, such as *The Country Dance*, were only rather hastily executed transfers. The frontispiece of Mallarmé's *Pages* (1891) is typical of the period during which the artist was under the strong influence of Ingres, and analysed, spell-bound, the stomach and the breasts of the *Source*. The *Portrait of Berthe Morisot, At Berneval*, the three variants of the *Pinned Hat*, and above all the *Two Bathers* (1895), *Mother and Child* and the two ravishing *Nudes* — true examples of sculpture in engraving — which adorn Duret's *History of the Impressionist Painters*, show with what sincere pleasure he furrowed the copper. Lithography, however seems to have been a medium better adapted to his genius.

It was with Degas as her printer, in the beginning of 1895, that Suzanne Valadon executed and drew her first soft-ground etching. The reasons which prompted Degas to advise this novice to use this particular process were, firstly, because it is speedy, and secondly, because it allows the original drawing to be preserved intact. Degas knew very well that with Suzanne there was no need to fear any compromise. He admired that stroke "*both hard and pliant,*" which feared nothing. He foresaw the effects of rugged beauty which this hand incapable of falsehood and this dauntless eye would extract from every material. And indeed, the whole process was revived by the terrible Maria. The printer was overwhelmed by the violence of the furrows that were dug in the zinc. The artist drove her strokes straight, as would a labourer, and the acid seething in the depths made them larger still. While it was in the grays, in light patches and semi-tints that the advocates of soft-ground etching generally achieved their triumphs, here we almost have the impression of a sculptor fixing the limit of planes, inventing profiles, and giving remarkable weight to every form, and especially to the nudes, which have the splendour and the hardness of marble.

What are the subjects of these plates ? Bathing scenes, children being dressed, servants drying themselves or doing their hair. Valadon always excelled in describing form, not piecemeal, but in all its unity. What strikes us most about her compositions, of which the austerity differs so much from that of Degas, is the tone; it is an imperative tone, like that of a mother who feigns severity in order to be better obeyed. There is an overwhelming passion under an apparent coldness, a tension which may be compared to a sense of duty; and there is charm, a charm so different from that pleasantness which is the privilege of the weaker sex, a bitter and sometimes sullen charm which colours everyday life with its angles, its wrinkles, its violence and its monotony. "Terrible Maria" only drew bodies deformed by age or servitude, children not plump and warm, but overgrown, angular and weedy. And yet she does not try to move us to pity by a facile pathos; she never complains, and it is by the stoicism of her stroke that our emotion is roused.

A first series of twelve zinc plates was engraved in 1896. It was not until 1904 or 1905 that the artist returned to engraving, and executed a few dry points. No weapon was better made to serve her. Valadon did not ask to be fondled : she penetrated the metal disdaining all rules, but to the advantage of expression. Taken by and large, her imperious technique has not changed since her first soft-ground etchings. Her many drawings and canvases, too, make one admire her absolute resistance to all influence, her uncompromising character and inspiration. Hers are genuine blocks, without fissure, blocks that will endure.

Together with these engravers the only name we could mention is that of Maurin, the too-neglected disciple of Degas and Lautrec, who contributed — just as much as Mary Cassatt, Pissarro (*The Farm at Eragny*) Béjot, Steinlen, Lepère, Boltini, and above all Rafaelli — to the fostering and renewal of the coloured print.

A barren period was soon in store for etching, which, with the exception of Forain, Naudin, Lepère, Steinlen, and some of the artists mentioned above, was only to be practised by second-rate hands. It was not until after the War that the importance of landscape painters such as Frelaut, Vergésarrat, Léopold Lévy, Beaufrère and Jacques Villon was discovered, previously they had been ignored by a public capable only of admiring insipid coloured prints, such as the Venices and the Versailles of the cheap bazaars, which look as though they had all passed through the same printer's hands and received the same greenish and russet brown tints.

THE RENAISSANCE OF LITHOGRAPHY IN BLACK AND WHITE AND OF COLOURED LITHOGRAPHY.

Towards 1890 lithography, which Fantin and Redon had never ceased to practise, suddenly came into favour again. The successive publication of the *Estampe Originale* and Vollard's *Peintres-Graveurs* had something to do with this resurrection. As a matter of fact it was above all colour that tempted the artists, who were fascinated by Chéret's posters and by the Japanese prints, and who discovered that the riches of the palette could have their equivalents on wood, copper or stone.

The example was set in 1874 by Manet, who executed his *Polichinelle* after a water-colour with the aid of seven stone plates. The true forerunner, however, was unquestionably Chéret. Colour, which his predecessors had outraged in their posters by combining it unsuccessfully with black, at last regained its freedom and charm. Even before he precisely defined the laws of chromolithography, Chéret instinctively joined a wash with the crayon, thereby opposing the transparent parts to the light parts and obtaining, thanks to his arbitrary imagination, a balance of forces in each composition. As though by accident and yet with a kind of prescience, he casts the high lights of his wash on to a fallen flower, a cymbal, the toe of a pump, while the rhythmic movements of dancing figures are defined by a vigorous, angular, frenzied and sometimes ragged stroke. His orchestration is erudite, with every value in harmony. Moreover by his practice of superimposing stone upon stone he produces those flat patches of red, blue, yellow and orange which stand out in contrast to the modulations made by crayon rubbings, to the spray effects and to the transparent stripes. It is to these contrasts between empty and filled-up spaces that his composition owes its solidity and depth. Soon every outline was to disappear. Contrasts of light and dark, of cold and warm colours are sufficient to indicate the position of the forms, which serve but as a charming pretext for colours in apposition or in contrast. In the inborn science of contrasting and complementary colours Chéret gave his imagination full play. In the hands of this comrade of the great Impressionists who, before Seurat, anticipated the laws of the breaking-up of light and optical blending, coloured lithography, hitherto laboured and monotonous, became an art. It was through Chéret and the Japanese engravings that the vision of painters was emancipated. On this point the testimonies of Puvis or of Monet are as convincing as those of Lautrec and of younger painters such as Bonnard, Vuillard, Roussel or Signac who all worked in Clot's studio about the year 1895. One cannot deny, of course, the importance of the part played by the printer in several of the coloured prints published by Vollard, admirable facsimiles produced with the collaboration of Renoir, Sisley, Cézanne and Guillaumin. Very often, however, it was an entirely original work, such as *La Sulamite* and *Beatrice* by Redon, the *Landscape* and *Intérieurs* by Vuillard, *Some Aspects of the Life of Paris* by Bonnard and some of the series ordered from Roussel, Maurice Denis, Dulac, Signac and Luce. Previously there had appeared the rather too anecdotal plates of Lewis Brown and Lunois. Engraving on copper, too, was occasionally enriched by the introduction of colour. Still, though Mary Cassatt, Pissarro, Maurin and Bottini have achieved undoubted success, it must be admitted that the coloured etching is exposed to dangers unknown in lithography. The process of etching, perilous enough as it is, becomes quite alarming when the preparation of the colouring matter for the different grains diverts the artist's mind from that which is essential, namely the distribution of bitten lines and the perfect harmony of ink and paper. The printer's part becomes predominant. Insipid colouring supplants the impressions pulled with the aid of reground copper plates; tone loses its candour, and the white of the sheet is deprived of its legitimate function. The etching is killed in its attempt to rival the picture. Thus it was that in spite of all the enthusiasm of Raffaelli, who founded the *Salon de l'Eau-forte en couleurs* in 1904, and in spite of a number of successes, coloured etching soon declined, and degenerated into productions of a cheap quality. The wood-cut, on the other hand, strong in tradition, ran into none of these dangers, and we shall see later what results in polychromy on wood were achieved by Henri Rivière, Lepère, Gauguin and the Beltrands.

However delightful were a number of coloured lithographs executed in this period — and we shall have occasion to return to them again — true connoisseurs will always show a preference for lithographs in black and white. Owing to a happy combination of circumstances a number of great painters — Toulouse-Lautrec, Degas, Renoir, Rodin, Gauguin, Forain, Maillol, Vuillard, and Bonnard — succumbed to the infectious charm of lithography in the last decade of the nineteenth century, and devoted to it a great part of their time and their inventive genius.

THE LITHOGRAPHS OF TOULOUSE-LAUTREC

These, together with those of Daumier, are the most magnificent work ever engraved on stone. It may seem strange perhaps, to join two masters so different in origin, education and temperament. Nevertheless, in both cases, the human being under its most familiar and earthly aspects became the object of such a burning curiosity that reality took on the magnitude of dreams. For indeed one may say without any fear of paradox that Lautrec was living in a dream in the middle of the appearance of reality lent him for so short a period. Nearly four hundred plates, of which about fifty are in colour, executed between 1892 and 1900, lead us to anticipate a work which, from the point of view of quantity, would undoubtedly have equalled that of Daumier. Like Daumier, Lautrec was gifted with the amazing visual memory, so indispensable to the lithographer, who cannot carry his stone about with him and must rely on his recollections if he is to avoid the chilly effect of the transfer. Lautrec saw and remembered. Everything became sharpened and purified in his imagination. He never felt himself so free as when bending over a stone which offered him, amid silence far away from the model, a surface more receptive than the marble tops of café tables, from which so many of his sketches were wiped out by the greasy cloth of the waiters.

It was in the printing-shops of Ancourt and Stern that he executed the most essential part of his works, that is to say, his lithographs. There is no need for us to repeat the mistake of certain light-hearted critics, who are never tired of drawing a contrast between Lautrec and Degas.

In the course of a long, sheltered life devoted to work, Degas delved deeper and deeper into the secrets of that technique of painting which Lautrec practised only by instinct. In his design Degas was for a long time indebted to the old masters, while Lautrec owed little to the museums. The contention often made by critics that Lautrec revenged himself on Nature for the deformities of his own body are surely due to a mental aberration incapable of distinguishing exaltation of character from a taste for ugliness. Lautrec was an analyst, not a chronicler; a poet, not a satirist; he was not, like Forain, a showman of human errors. When he underlined the odious aspect of a situation or a type of man, he never sought refuge in *chiaroscuro*; he never had the inclination, like Degas, to contaminate fairyland, or to bring hatred and malice into the marvellous. Design for him was truly an act of adoration. Everything that concerns the human being filled him with joy, and every manifestation of character, however exaggerated, was for him a source of wonder and excitement. It has never been sufficiently emphasised that it was the inner life that inspired the ecstasies of this fanatic in his wanderings from street to street, from bar to bar, from theatre to theatre, from one house of ill-fame to another. The majority of his works show a hidden tendency towards portraiture. The comedy which he builds up is not limited to a few elementary personalities and set situations. He always makes use of the particular in his description of the general. He observes every individual with infinite respect, or perhaps, if the word respect may sound paradoxical, with infinite curiosity; he wonders at the conditions in which circumstances have placed him, at the state of life which he leads, at the deformities which age and surroundings have inflicted upon him, but he goes beyond these outward appearances. For observing his models he chooses a position from which he may surprise them in the middle of their daily occupations, when they are ignorant of the fact that they are being observed and can reveal at the same time all that is most unstable and most lasting in them. To judge the works of Lautrec, however, solely from the point of view of the picturesque effect of their colouring and their situations would be to falsify their spirit. We must forget the theatre, the music hall, the red salon, with all their ornaments and accessories, and realise that his favourite models — dancing girls, comediennes, and prostitutes — are characters far more complex than we imagine at first sight, before we have seen the transfiguration wrought by the hand of the great artist who makes them live again in our eyes, lovable in the sense which that word had of old, and who reveals the stuff from which these smiles, these postures of the head, these inclinations and silences are made, which could easily have been the smiles and postures of goddesses, saints, or empresses.

Lautrec signed his first posters in 1892 — *The Glutton at the Moulin Rouge*, *The Hanged Man*, *The Japanese Divan*, *Bruant*, *Reine de Joie*, etc. — thus he was initiated into the practice of lithography which Chéret had used to adorn so many private collections in Paris. The Japanese prints, which appeared at the same time as these fantasies, continued to upset the conventions. Through them distortion was made systematic; the orthodox suddenly found itself dethroned; set rules regarding the representation of shadows and the sun's course were no longer observed; bold and delicate effects of colour and in the setting of a page, the familiar reverence for all the rhythms in life, for the most humble and artless objects, all these awoke in Lautrec a fascination to which he delighted to give free rein. He brought colour to the art of the lithographer, and his first attempts were almost posters *(The Glutton and her Sister, The Englishman of the Moulin Rouge)* ; he quickly came to the conclusion that formal groups and heavy contrasts in mural decoration were dangerous elements in small compositions intended to be viewed at close range. The arbitrary splendour with which so many of his works executed in 93 are endowed soon gives way to a less uniform line and to subtler harmonies. The book jackets designed for *Vieilles Histoires* (1893), pulled in black, recall the poster and the pen and ink drawings of Hokusai. The outlines are in pencil, in strong line, completely black, in contrast to the vigorous whites that stand out against the back-ground. But his stroke soon became more supple; the crayon, more vigorous, more delicate than the pencil, is joined with a wash. Where once there had only been stains, the painted form stands out in relief; the same evolution can be observed in the work of Bonnard and Vuillard. The technique of the " *crachis* " is summed up in the *Café-Concert* or *Escarmouche* series. The complete Lautrec is to be seen already in his first portrait of *Yvette Guilbert*, a simple profile, treated in such a way, by contrasts of intensity, as to convey all the facial characteristics. There is the same delicacy of touch in *En Quarante*. By lessening the importance of the dulled surfaces, by toning down the contrast between high lights and low ones, softening all shadows, clarifying the " *crachis* ", Lautrec, with the help of the tooth-brush always to be found in his pocket, would spread a kind of fine rain, luminous and ashy grey, over the face of Oenone, when, white as marble, Phaedra (Sarah Bernhardt) appears before her. On a lip, a lock of hair, the lace of a woman's corsage or the toe of a shoe, the stick of charcoal places a discreet touch of black, so as to accentuate and heighten the effects of the greys and the whites. Nearly all these prints have as their theme life on the stage or in the promenade : the Théâtre Français, Théâtre Libre, Folies-Bergères, Moulin-Rouge, Gaité-Rochechouart. This gnome has acquired wings. He already excels in finding that balance, characteristic of his art, between the elements of caricature and the poetic elements, and in interpreting with magic subtlety a subject which is often burlesque and contains an unexpected element. *(Rejane et Galipaux dans Madame Sans-Gêne, Ida Heath au hoa*, etc...)

It is probable that the introduction of Whistler's lithographs made an impression on Lautrec. These little masterpieces, impressions lightly thrown on the stone, scarcely inked, distinct at the same time as intangible, encouraged him not definitely to abandon the high lights made with pencil and wash, but to localise the effects and only to use them prudently. Lautrec's vision was not yet sufficiently sharpened to describe Yvette Guilbert or Marcelle Lender in all their rôles; every element of comic disharmony is, as it were, transfigured by the witty sensuality with which he conveys a look, a smile, a shoulder, a hand, a back, a greeting, a step or a dance, and with which he suggests the marvellous delicacy of movement of the figure of an actress or a ballerine on tip-toe. On the stone itself there is a rival play produced by a peculiar transposition of lines and values, which belong to reality and at the same time to a dream world, and which achieve a harmony not only in the attitude and the expression, but also in the balance and the contrasts which are established between the lines and the centres of light. We are enchanted by the qualities of truthfulness and charm which we find in *Cécy Loftus*, with her tipsy air, her little top hat, humming a refrain as though she meant it as an insult, in *May Belford* waving a greeting, or in *Mlle Pois Vert*.

Never had such a determined pencil moved so lovingly over the stone. So that no unforeseen accident should mar his work, the artist carefully supervised the quality of the granite, and chose the paper and the ink he needed, varying the shades in turn — gray-green, chestnut-gray, and gray-black. It seems as if the " beaux-noirs " so cherished by lithographers, the contrasts between velvety surfaces and large patches of pure white of which the romantics were so proud, came too easily to this hand, whose owner wished to play an unaccompanied air. Thus there are the *Portraits of Actors and Actresses* and the series of masterpieces dated 1896, of which the prototype, perhaps, is *Ida Heath en tutu*, with her left leg thrust higher than her head, and with her arms, parallel, falling back in direction, Ida Heath dancing with an effort full of careful grace and liveliness, the absolute black of her bodice and of the little bows on her shoulders emphasising the lightness of her fair hair and the spangles on the tulle. *The Box at the Theatre* (Faust), *Supper in London*, *White and Black*, are all masterpieces of movement used with economy, in which the slightest touch has its weight, its value, and almost its perfume.

In the same year (1896) another important series was produced in which colour, which had so long been proscribed, came into its own again. The underlying conception here is quite different from that behind the first lithographs. Lautrec had realised by then that in polychromy, just as much as in engraving in black and white, everything can be expressed in the most moderate fashion. The pencil is only used to add a light touch here and there in order to affirm a contour or the density of a surface; the framework of the design can still be seen through the gentle rain of many colours. The vigorous cuts of his earlier engravings and his flat tints are discarded for this fleeting play of colours and these elusive vibrations, the white sheet of paper being a kind of playground for myriads of tiny little drops. Lautrec discovered his own equivalent for the dot effect of the Impressionists, just as Pissarro had found it in the grain of the aquatint. He believed in contrasting his tones, and did not super-impose them one upon another. It would be impossible to overestimate either the quality of the harmonies invented by Lautrec, a quality already apparent in his posters and programmes, or the reserve with which he made use of high lights, as though he foresaw the abuse which was later made of them by so many other engravers influenced by himself. The most remarkable plates of the *Elles* series are perhaps those printed in one tone only, a good example being *Lassitude*. As a prelude to this series of studies of the life of women in their homes which were conceived in quite a different sentiment from that with which Degas and Forain regarded bed-rooms and dressing-rooms — came the *Sleep*, a masterpiece in which we can almost hear the breathing of the model, and where the moulding of the face, the breast, and even of the hands is brought out by an outline so simple and so pure that we are reminded not only of the drawings of the eighteenth century, with which the vigorous quality of the print has much in common, but also of the most perfect types of the female nude produced by the Venetians and the Greeks. We then come, in the year 1897, to *The Great Box at the Theatre*, *The Clown at the Moulin-Rouge*, *Princely Idyll*, *The Dance at the Moulin-Rouge*, *The Little Box at the Theatre* and the *Country Expedition*, in which the harmonies are brought out with a taste and perfection never equalled on the coloured engraving of any other country except, perhaps, Japan, harmonies concise both in analysis and in feature, and displayed to the greatest advantage in the amazing portrait of *Elsa the Viennese*.

There are other masterpieces of the same period which owe nothing to polychromy. We have a fine example in *To the Mouse*, where a new subject is the dog; — this animal, seldom treated by Lautrec before, was brought into the foreground for the first time. From now on we shall see dogs of many breeds — bulldogs, mongrels, and fox terriers — sharing in the gambols of horses and men. A masterly series of lithographs of race-course scenes (*The Paddock*, *The Jockey reaching the Goal*, *The Trainer*, *Amazone et Tonneau*, *The Old Horse*, and others) shows a complete understanding of all that lives and breathes, and a truly classical certainty and simplicity, in spite of that lack of balance to which the artist was soon to succumb.

We can imagine the heights to which such a work might have developed had not death so arbitrarily cut it short. The artist's powers of imagination, stimulated by different causes and lavished on whatever he undertook, a book-cover, a title-heading to a piece of music, an invitation card or a programme, and the constant excitement aroused by his observation of himself and his fellow-men, were now enriched by new elements. There were many signs to show that Lautrec was soon to abandon his favourite surroundings, to change his observation posts — the café table, the theatre stalls, the actress's dressing-room, and the gallery — and to discover other lights than those of the foot-lights and the spot-lights, other perspectives than those of the stage, other pastimes than venal love. In the illustrations which he was commissioned to produce for the *Histoires Naturelles*, it was with gentle lyricism that he blended the poetry of natural elements with the life of man's animal friends ; in those portraits which surpass the works of Jules Renard he rediscovered the artless-ness of La Fontaine. While those swift impulses of boyish bluster were still to be observed in many improvised sketches, a new seriousness seemed to have come over him; his models acquired an unexpected tragic aspect. I am referring not only to the faces of actresses which he drew in about 1898, but also to that most admirable portrait of a woman wasted by satiety of pleasure, who looks as though she has been riveted for years to the same bench, but still finds strength enough to smile, with sweet and steady eyes. from under a mass of feathers and tulle. In the plate entitled *To the Cockchafer* the fairylike colouring of silvery dust seems almost magical, and brings out to its full value the one dark spot in the whole picture : the gentle frisking of the little animal squatting in a devoted attitude by the side of its mistress.

The lithographs of Lautrec represent our national genius at its best. Never, since some of the drawings of the eighteenth century, has anything better balanced or more subtle been produced by a combination of wit, taste and observation. There are some masters whose prints seem to be merely works of a preparatory character, or nothing more than a pastime. Lautrec's work was also a pastime, but a pastime which was essential. When we look at these designs, of which only a few impressions were made, as if to accentuate their aristocratic character, we find ourselves in the midst of an immense creative work, which is still too recent for us to appreciate at its true value.

THE PORTRAITS BY EUGÈNE CARRIÈRE
THE LITHOGRAPHS BY RENOIR, GAUGUIN, AND MAILLOL

Carrière, after his earlier efforts at commercial lithography, as for instance some two or three title-headings to popular music, did not return to engraving till about 1890. In his *Newly-born Child in a Bonnet* we have the first example of his use of scraper, glass-paper, pencil and wash, producing that peculiar technique of erasure which he later perfected in his great portraits. Alphonse Daudet, his daughters Nelly, Elise, and Marguerite, Edmond de Goncourt, Verlaine, Rochefort, and Puvis de Chavannes emerge, one by one, from the darkness, and we are at a loss to find out where the light comes from, as though its source were in the subjects themselves. Very light pencil strokes mould the lips and the eye-lids, like shadows on marble or on wax, yet so precise that the slightest subtleties of plane are defined as in sculpture. Like flames coming out of the night, there flash glimpses of a mo-ther's forehead as she clasps her child, of an artist at work on his clay, of a miner in the fumes of smoke, or of a foundry-man in the middle of streams of gold.

In collaboration with the printer Duchâtel, Carrière tried his hand at a succession of prints in an attempt to find an equivalent to that play of chiaroscuro which was the distinctive feature of his paintings. He traced his design, transferred it to a second stone, and printed it in a more sustained tone. By this method he succeeded in producing those deep, velvety blacks which contrast with the transparent grays achieved by means of a scraper or by rubbing with a cloth. All his faces, without exception, stand out against a background which reflects the darkness of night. It would perhaps be better to say that they are linked with this background, which is itself throbbing with life, the reserve of all strength and all gesture, the link between mind and matter. Without ever imprisoning form in the fetters of an outline, Carrière succeeds in defining with admirable authority the various characteristics of a forehead, a temple, a cheek, or an eyebrow, and although it is only the face that is shown us, with light focused on the centres of thought, we can create the entire being in our imagination. " He will have to make his confession, " Carrière said about one of his models. Every model is the scene of an immense conflict : the soul breathes through the apertures of the outer face of man, fashioning it from inside, while the light of day moulds it from outside. " A face is not a cast, " Carrière once said ; " it is a statue of bronze, hammered and sculptured from within. " I should like to apply this remark, which has been abused for twenty years, to the author of the lithographs *Verlaine* and *Lisbeth*, as well as to the work of Cézanne and Seurat. In the art of sacrifice no artist went further than Carrière, who cared nothing for the sensual aspect of things and for all second-rate intrigue. No portraits have a greater depth than his.

*

There is an irresistible charm about the portraits which Renoir designed on stone — *Diéterle* (or *The Lady in the big Hat*), *Wagner*, *Rodin*, *Cézanne*, *Pierre Renoir as a Child* — though their production was more hasty and they were often taken from a canvas. Renoir's work surpasses the great coloured lithographs of Clot, which, though they have the velvety effect of pastels, are nevertheless only interpretations. In prints like *The Bather*, *The two pinned Hats*, *The Children playing with a Ball*, *The Child with a Biscuit*, portraits done with the aid of light pearly rubbings and moist touches with the brush, Renoir introduces touches which are known to him alone. There is an animation and a natural charm in every one of his works, by which success is achieved almost without any preparatory effort on the artist's part. We admire the fullness of the volumes, the ease of movement, and that exquisite harmony between inner content and outer form, which enabled Renoir to arrest the flight of fading charms and to lend an aspect of permanence even to the least studied of his prints.

It was in 1889 that Gauguin executed a series of lithographs done after the paintings from his first journey to Martinique, as well as those he did at Pont-Aven and Arles. They were printed on saffron-coloured paper. These zincographs, which preceded his wood-cuts, are characteristic of his " synthetic " period, full of large flat patches and deliberate circles. These first attempts have not as much character as *Manao Tupapau*, a masterpiece engraved in the interval between two sojourns in Tahiti and published in the *Estampe Originale*. In fashioning the body of this dusky Olympia, lying in a hut scintillating with sparks as mysterious as those which flicker in the lithographs of Redon, Gauguin adopted his favourite technique of erasure. Every resource that stone possesses helped to build up this plate, which was only to be followed by one other, inspired by a Maori virgin. In those admirable wood-cuts to which Gauguin later devoted his talents, one could almost say that he continued to use the technique of a lithographer.

It is indeed unfortunate that the engravings of Puvis de Chavannes are so few in number. *Normandy*, the *Young Girl in a big Hat*, and especially the traced drawing of *The Poor Fisherman*, show what an excellent medium stone provided for rendering the grays of Puvis in all their serene nobility.

Rodin's *New Idol*, which came after his dry points, was likewise an unparallelled success. While the illustrations of the *Garden of Tortures* were done from watercolours traced on stone, in this print we have two forms penetrating into one another like shadow and daylight. The friendship which existed between Rodin and Carrière seems to assert itself in this unique plate, in which the sculptor of *The Kiss* obtains similar effects to those of the lithographer of *Verlaine*.

Aristide Maillol, in a number of wood-cuts and lithographs produced from 1895 onwards under the combined influence of Renoir and the Symbolists, showed signs of that unity of form and that completeness which are such striking characteristics of his sculptures.

BONNARD, VUILLARD, AND DENIS

Pierre Bonnard, who was trying his hand at everything — posters, furniture, screens, theatrical decoration — felt himself attracted by stone at about the same time as Toulouse-Lautrec. Ancourt printed his first poster in colour, *France-Champagne*, reminiscent of Chéret's style, as well as many prints showing the Japanese influence in their unexpected page-setting and the freshness of their colouring set out in flat patches, without shadow or relief.

The lucidity of the *Small familiar Scenes*, a series of lithographs which illustrate nineteen songs by Claude Terrasse (whose *Petit Solfège* he had already illustrated before), is sometimes spoilt by abbreviations and caricature-like distortions. The plastic and poetic quality of these prints, however, is really novel. Pen or brush create form anew, and lend an unusual aspect to the living models, to still life, and to landscapes (*La chanson du Grand-Père*, *Morning Prayer*, *Reveries*, *Horsewoman* and others). Bonnard soon disciplined his fantasy and tempered down his unconformities and that exuberance to which, in spite of all, the productions of his youthful period owe part of their charm (*The Dogs*, *Nude*). Other examples of this first phase are a programme for *L'Œuvre*, and some covers for the *Théâtre des Pantins* and for the *Lithographie en couleurs* of Mellerio.

It was in 1900 that Verlaine's *Parallèlement* was published by Vollard, a volume which for a long time was scorned by book connoisseurs. The freedom with which these arabesques were scattered over the margins without any apparent justification, in each and every free space, seemed at the time to be as audacious as the immodesty of the text. Since the publications of the romantic age and Delacroix's *Faust* lithography had only rarely been associated with the printed page. The *Histoires Naturelles*, coming after the *Au Pied du Sinaï* had alone ventured to demonstrate that it was a process which could be easily adapted to the types of the printing-press. It was with childish joy that Bonnard imposed his exhilarating fantasies on the surface of the stone. His pencil, so delicately applied, evokes a pleasure akin to that called up by the art of Whistler and Lautrec. One might call it illustration in verse, a subdued accompaniment that follows without effort the rhythm of each poem and unwinds the music of naked forms around the body of the baby-faun.

Daphnis et Chloé, published in 1902, is perhaps the most beautifully illustrated book since the eighteenth century. Following the text step by step, Bonnard's genius displays itself with profuse lavishness. It is indeed astonishing to realise that less than a year has sufficed for the production of these hundred and sixty lithographs, vignetted, conjuring up successively seascapes or woodland scenes, grottoes, harbours, public places, the interior of a farmhouse or a palace, people clothed or in the nude, playing the flute amidst a flock of sheep with dogs, or carrying on that sweet duet, the preliminaries and whimsies of which provide the justification for the book itself. In no way nonplussed by his task of bringing antiquity to life again, Bonnard has rediscovered effortlessly the atmosphere of those happy days. The roguishness which reveals itself elsewhere in his art, and which has at times led him along strange ways, is here subordinated to a sense of balance of which one would hardly have thought him capable.

The lithographs of *Daphnis* precede, as it were, his mature works, when, now master of his art, Bonnard gives free expression to those delightful movements which sometimes give him the risk of losing the actual meaning of his form. He is absorbed by the reinvention of a colour scheme. The very technique displayed in his lithographs lends to their charm and accentuates their delicacy. The presence of a very faint printing process accentuates, too, the sensuous dream that lingers long after we have closed the book. *Daphnis* betrays the same unconcern as *Parallèlement* and the set of coloured lithographs entitled *Some Aspects of Paris Life*, in which the attractive incidents and scenes in a great city make a painter happy, in whose eyes a dog, or a hat provide problems to be solved, and mysteries to fathom. Showers of rain on the boulevards or bridges of Paris, from the fifth storey we look down upon the teeming street or, from the balcony stalls, on the audience in the pit. Certain plates tell the story of the joys of boating or the green harmony of a garden. In these works, many of which have appeared in the *Painters Engravers*, all the changing moods and infinite variety of Bonnard's art appear triumphantly. They were so little understood that the artist, as did the majority of his contemporaries, lost interest for the time being in process-work as such and in the printed book itself.

**
*

Vuillard's first lithographs indicate the subjects which attract him most (*The Kitchen, The Window*). Executed about 1893, no impressions of them have been taken. A series of small drawings on stone will shortly adorn the catalogue of the Exhibition of *La Dépêche* (where Vuillard is rubbing shoulders with Bonnard, Anquetin, Maurin and Serrusiet), the supplements of the *Revue Blanche* or the instalments of *L'Epreuve* : a pencil-drawing, a wash-drawing testifying to the poetical feeling in small bourgeois homes, the friendly half-light surrounding young women trying-on hats, sewing, laying table-cloths. The unexpectedness with which the letterpress, too, drawn in pencil, plays a decorative part, adds to the charm of the programmes designed for Lugné Poë. Was it through modesty or the fear of squandering his powers that Vuillard never consented to illustrate a book ? That is to be deplored above all, but his gifts of analyse, his scruples, and the intensity with which he has recreated the intimate light of a period compensate for this omission. All the same, one wishes that he would have followed the example of Odilon Redon and Renoir and have allowed reproductions of his portraits to be printed on stone. Besides those monochromatic lithographs where extremely irridescent greys, broken up by the use of the scraper, are intermingled with rich blacks (*The Box at the Theatre*), Vuillard has issued a score of colour prints unusually harmonious in tone. On backgrounds of flat colour-wash, of dull or clear tone, his pencil strokes convey their suggestions of graining. The artist has returned rapidly to a more oriental conception of printing. The economies on the earlier plates, the broad strokes so flatly conceived disappear and that which remains savours too much of the poster. In his small prints Vuillard reintroduces the feeling of the depth and play of light and shade ; broken-up tones intensify; rose-grey, rose-gold, beige, maroon, blue-grey, offer contrast to the tonic accents placed here and there. A section of the set of twelve plates, issued by Vuillard about 1898, portray the life of humble homes, views of little communicating rooms enlivened by the comings and goings of the inmates. Walls are covered with various kinds of paper, and we discover the quiet harmony of fitments and everyday furniture which control the daily round. Everything there is of charm and of depth of vision in the art of Vuillard finds expression in this series, but unfortunately without any to-morrow. Like Bonnard and K.-X. Roussell, who, in an unpublished set of dusty, sunlit landscapes, as volatile as pastels, makes greens, yellows and soft pink colours vibrate between the whites that soften them ; like Maurice Denis, whose sketch-book *Amours*, steeped in a perfume of artless mysticism, forms with Dulac's *Song of Songs* an essential document of the symbolistic period in art ; like Henri Rivière, who, aided by Verneau the printer, thanks to certain lessening of depth by the use of lighter inks on the roller, obtained effects recalling those of his bluish woods (*Aspects of Nature, Parisian Landscapes, The Fairy of Hours, The 36 Views of the Eiffel Tower*) ; like Valloton, Luce, Signac, Gros, Anquetin, d'Espagnat, Ranson, Seguin, Ch. Guérin or the delightful Serret, who only made too brief an incursion into the world of printing, Vuillard too gave up for a considerable time the delights of lithography. The splendid impulse in coloured lithography, summed up by Mellerio in a brilliant treatise, suddenly stopped. As regards lithography in black and white, apart from the fine portraits of Odilon Redon, certain heads by Belleroche, Guiguet, Henri Bataille, J.-E. Blanche, E. Laurent, and certain landscapes and still lifes of Le Sidaner and a number of comic drawings, between 1900 and 1917, one wonders which great names will continue to live.

THE LITHOGRAPHS AND ETCHINGS OF FORAIN

It was sometime in 1890 that Jean-Louis Forain, who until then had only engraved the frontispieces to *Martha* and the plates of *Croquis Parisiens* (1880), turned to the medium of lithography. He soon, like Whistler, became his own printer, selecting his own paper and inks, so that each plate, from which only a few impressions were taken (fifty as a maximum, sometimes from two to fifteen), produced proofs sensibly differing one from the other. If the craze in America, inclined to regard the lithographer's as an inferior art, tended towards the etcher's, for us, on the other hand, Forain has never expressed better his own temperament and times than in those beautiful series which, quite naturally, classify themselves in *Private Rooms, Boxes at the Theatre, Behind the Scenes, Toilets, Court-room Scenes* and *Strike Scenes*. The inspiration, generally speaking, is imprisoned in those localities where men and women seek one another, find doleful companionship in an atmosphere charged with tragedy. Endowed with an irresistible feeling for action, able to detach a scene (in every sense of the word, and, especially in that which women love to give it), to select the critical moment, Forain, even as Octave Mirbeau, whom he was born to illustrate, reduced humanity to certain fixed types, though simple enough psychologically speaking. Three or four settings suffice for him to set his comedy. We often find him reproducing the same theme, the recapitulation of an old grievance for example (there are no less than ten versions of *Friction after the Bath*). These prints bear no captions; we have to supply them for ourselves. The style too is controversial : it slaps us in the face, is insulting. The light and shade, so often employed by Daumier, and Carrière after him, for the delicate harmonising of lines, is present as an impartial intermediary. There may be something theatrical in this mode of procedure. Forain's line sometimes seems to be arbitrarily fixed; he gives us the impression of reconstructing in a studio, a studied theme, and that his zest expends itself coldly on puppets. It is impossible, nevertheless, to deny him the weight which his compositions carry, the assured evidence which they convey especially between 1890-1900, How they have already been able to change the outlines of the politician (type of Arthur Meyer), the artist, the business man with mutton-chop whiskers and a moustache or an umbrella, chewing a cigar ! The woman is always depicted as a hunted creature, selling herself joylessly. All those appurtenances which, as one finds with Lautrec, had the delicacy borrowed from the Japanese school — bath-robe, serviette, bottles, soap, tooth-brush, hair-brush — everything adorable in the Eternal She — the bath-room as well as the chair or the chimney-piece — all appear tragic, hostile, worn-out. A suggestion of fairyland illumines the floors of the stage, the pirouettes of the ladies of the ballet, as portrayed by Degas; here auditorium, wings, boxes display the poverty, the monotony of a calling lit up by no illusions. The same hopeless gestures are repeated. And just as Forain raises the tone when, as in his *Strike Scenes* he shows the orator, erect on his dais, stirring up a crowd of workmen, or as he depicts on a plate that heralded the moving series of 1914-1918 (*In Greece*, 1897), the desolation caused by the war, or when he presents, in his series of *Scenes in the Court-room*, the big " Guard " controlling the crowd, the homeless mother and her children, we feel ourselves wounded by this lack of fellow-feeling, this wish to degrade, this vitriolic enthusiasm, such as we inhale from Mirbeau, Bloy, Tailhade.

These lithographs are nevertheless counted as among the most powerful of the 19th century. The lack of restraint, often broken off abruptly, that gives to the parallel contour-lines or hatchings the feeling of a succession of fierce injuries, this art of massing shadow round the figures, of creating a forbidding pathos, allows these creations to surpass, without any doubt whatsoever, any pen or pencil drawings, and to show to what extent the artist has gained in breadth of style compared with his design which hitherto had hardly more density than can be found in the work of Somm or Grévin.

*
* *

What was the inspiration that induced Forain, who had not looked at a copperplate since his youthful essays, to turn once more to etching in 1908 or thereabouts ? At that time, without abandoning the subjects so dear to lithographers, his inspiration appears to have broken loose from the naturalistic atmosphere which pervades the first part of his work. Rembrandt and Daumier became his mentors in succession to Degas and Lautrec. They did not succeed in communicating to him anything more than the illusion of sympathy. At the approach of old age, Forain turned to the Bible for help; yet in the Holy Book he found no more than a " History " similar to all others : here a criminal action, there an " affaire ". He unmasks the traitor, the executioner, the wicked thief; he would meet Jesus face to face, but this Jesus refused him.

This new grandeur to which Forain now aspires is not exempt from artifice and scholasticism. He plays havoc with his pictures, cutting across them in an arbitrary manner, and overburdening them in order to increase their pathos. The more he works on a plate, the more it loses the sincerity of its earlier stages. There are etchings, however, such as *After the Apparition*, which lingers in our memory owing to that large space left empty in the centre of the plate, *The Meeting under the Vault*, *The Morsel of Bread*, and the series inspired by the Prodigal Son — which all show the effort he makes, sometimes without success, at achieving a serene atmosphere contrary to his nature, and at rising from the mire in order to find power elsewhere than in violence, and acquire a certainty other than that bred by bitterness.

The scarceness of his etchings, of which only a few copies were made, justify the favour they enjoyed. It is indeed his engravings that are more likely to assure a lasting fame for Jean Louis Forain than his paintings, whose subject matter is confused and often loud, and which suffer from a melodramatic distribution of lights which lends too arbitrary an effect to the livid faces which emerge from the darkness and recall Daumier and Rembrandt.

THE HUMORISTS : WILLETTE, STEINLEN, LEANDRE, JEAN VEBER, POULBOT

Killed by the invention of photomechanic processes, original lithography little by little disappeared from the satirical papers where its splendour had been so well asserted. It looked as though the period of artists like Daumier and Gavarni had come to an end, and political cartoons seemed to have been definitely abandoned. An outburst of passions had certainly been aroused by the Dreyfus case, but in neither of the opposed camps did Forain, Caran d'Ache, Steinlen, or Hermann Paul make use of the lithographer's pencil. Many of them regretted, however, that their ephemeral fantasies, wasted as they were on dailies and weeklies, had to suffer from the deadening effects of stereotype.

The paintings of Willette have all those distinctive features which are proper to the lithographer. He was sentimental like Gavarni, inquisitive about all things concerning women, impulsive, waggish, tender-hearted, and egoistic. He dwelt between Heaven and Earth, in attics or on the Paris embankment, and created a world fashioned after his own image, puerile, charming, full of allegories and dreams, of good fairies and evil bogeys. Reviving the old type of dance subjects, this romantic urchin created two types : the little woman of Montmartre — working girl, model, or grisette — doomed to die as the grasshopper, and the pantomine Pierrot who resembles her like a brother. His lithographs, worked with fine, short and feverish strokes, rendered lighter still by means of the scraper, have a graceful charm. While the drawing is often too stylish (and this is an inborn defect of all illustrators), it has a sincere sensuality and a kind of epic fantasy which raise him to the level of a poet among lithographers, often achieving his greatest successes in small-sized works like menus, covers, or vignettes.

Steinlen, whom Willette had introduced to the Chat Noir in 1883, was attracted by every type of drawing. Supported by the example of Daumier and by his own innate generosity, he soon abandoned the anecdote, the atmosphere of the Embankment and the air of the reckless libertine. It was the street that obsessed him — with all its contrasts, its perspectives, its lights, and its everyday tragedy. His strokes resemble the strokes of Carrière : they envelop the forms, as though defending and protecting them. There is a note of optimism about his pictures of human suffering and the War-time atmosphere. He is fond of great symbolic figures, soaring over the crowds of humanity. A lover of cats and stray dogs and of all those homeless ones who have fallen by the wayside, he sings a song of comfort in his etchings and lithographs, which brings joy to the crossroads and makes the tramp's heavy sack feel lighter on his back. The sincerity of his sentiment enabled him to acquire a firmness which was lacking in his design. His etchings, which date later than his lithographs, abound in contrasts and are bitten vigorously, but they are inclined to be heavy.

Leandre is fond of dull greys whose softness is in strange contrast with those deformed figures of his, a mannerism which became fashionable ever since the artists of the *Charivari* had evolved the style of enormous heads balanced on dwarf bodies. The sentimentality of this lithographer is curiously reconciled to this grotesque freakishness which affects every feature of the figures he designed.

The cripples, barbers, bowl-players, and ogres of Jean Veber linger in the memory by the extravagance of their gestures. He owes his fame to his paintings and to his coloured lithographs, but he is really better in the art of black and white. Prints in one colour — such as *Public Opinion, Progress, We Bear Our Dead,* which are less known than *The Extractor of Teeth* or the *Game of Cock-Farthing* — show with what lyric feeling, inspired by Raffet, Goya, and Brueghel, he could instil life into his symbols and reveal the epic character of his little scenes of middle-class life, his landscapes, and his pictures of fairyland, in which all his figures are but the personifications of a few primordial instincts, of a few senseless paradoxes of the universe. The more grotesque his subject, the deeper becomes his lyric feeling. With that great courage and violence to which men of tender sentiment so often rise, he was almost alone of all the artists of the beginning of this century who did not hesitate in casting his merciless regard on social and political life, in denouncing the oppression of the masses, held down either by the whip or by specious oratory, and in lacerating the oppressors. The War, which he foretold in *The Revenants* (1911), was to provide him with new models : the number of the blind and mutilated becomes multiplied as time goes on. Ten years after the Armistice, slowly suffocated by gas and fully conscious that no hope was left for him, Jean Veber departed from this world without uttering one word of complaint.

That fulness of scope which the progress of lithography acquired thanks to the work of Lautrec and Forain attracted other talented artists who were influenced by them in a greater or lesser degree, such as Hermann Paul, Ibels, Abel Faivre, Neumont, and others. A little later a new fosterling of the Embankment made his name by resurrecting the type of the urchin, the perspectives of steep lanes peopled with tiny human beings, a poetry of his own that gives off a strong smell of asphalt. That was Poulbot, in every way an adopted son of Willette's.

BERNARD NAUDIN

François Courbin was the first to teach Naudin engraving, and to acquaint him with the works of Abraham Bosse, Rembrandt, Callot, and Goya at the Cabinet des Estampes. The authority which Naudin's design inspires, with the Indian ink outlines often set off with wash, the fulness and intensity of his stroke, drawn with a steel nib or a quill, all tell of a born engraver. We may add to these qualities the nobility of his deliberately archaic style, his elegance and proud eloquence, and that sense of ornament which he displayed in many of his works and which caused his name to be attached to the peculiar style which he originated.

Master in a craft which he never considered as a purpose in itself, but always as a means of rendering that chamber music which is the print, Naudin purposely cast aside all the slipshod trickeries which are the favoured weapons of the weak and which tend to compromise sincerity of design. If, about 1903 and 1904, he sometimes made use of aquatint in his first sketches on copper or zinc, which he modestly entitled " learner's attempts," he did so with the same discretion as a Goya or a Manet. Very soon, however, he altogether abandoned that method of colouring and sought to derive all the effects he needed from simple etching with the help of the dry point and the burin.

When we observe the violence with which the acid has attacked the metal in his prints, we can well say that the etching, which is so often weak in other hands, here rightly deserves its name of *aqua fortis.* In order to define the character of

56

Naudin's work we must begin by explaining his method and the passion with which this artist who was also a musician (and that is why one feels tempted to use musical expressions when speaking of his work) arranges his orchestration : that is to say, his method of biting. First of all he makes the essential features, as it were the very soul of the design, come out gradually on a transparent coating of varnish, and then we see him enter into the mysterious domain of *execution*. The point, which he handles as firmly as he would a pen, furrows the metal at times as if it were a burin, and at times scarcely touches it at all. The second stage of orchestration comes when the hour of the acid arrives. Naudin had no use for the customary practice of plunging the metal plate in the bath and taking it out again after the first biting. This classical method seemed to him to be too elementary. As we watch him deposit, one after another, the drops of acid on his copper plate by means of a brush, we are inclined to say, as we would of a painter, that in one place he has stayed its action, while in another he prolonged it. In order to add to the resonance of this or that black, he makes some of the furrows wider. Every plate is thus treated in its own way, without uniformity, and whichever part we look at, we are aware of the active life which animates it.

This vital character of his biting tends to increase the pathetic qualities of the personages whom his imagination brings to life. Through on a few occasions he handled political subjects. (*Irons, Death by Shooting*, or *The Shooting Squad*), he usually preferred to eliminate from every action or setting all that is particular or topical, and to concentrate on the eternal. It is nearly always in the portrayal of misery that his richest qualities are displayed. While others are fond of handling gold and sumptuous garments, it is the decisive folds of misshapen clothes that inspire him, objects worn with much use, immovable and everlasting, kitchen utensils, musical instruments, and workshop tools. It is the poorest faces that he finds most eloquent, faces which disease, excess, or privation have reduced to their essential features, thin, emaciated, and gnarled, faces which have become frightful and nameless like the skeletons they are going to be to-morrow. Gustave Geffroy was the first to emphasise the " deathly elegance " of these compositions. Although invisible, Death stalks about everywhere in his works, not toothless and satanic, but an unavoidable and almost comforting presence. Who would not recognise it in his beautiful blacks ?

Almost at the same time as Jean-Louis Forain, Bernard Naudin turned to the Bible for the themes of his most beautiful etchings, and brought back among men Him Who shared in all their trials and the Mother of All Suffering (*The Virgin and the Labourers*, 1907; *Christ and the Bohemians*, 1901; *The Small Nativity with bare Feet*, 1912). Two recurrent themes keep coming up again and again in his work, and provide it with new enlightenment and inspiration. Firstly, there is music : a gateway to deliverance and to dreams, which opens out into the skies, its keys being guitars, hurdy-gurdies, violins, and barrel-organs (*The Dwarf Woman with the Violins* and two admirable plates entitled *The Guitar Player in a Caravan* and *The Beggar with a Hurdy-Gurdy*). Secondly, there is childhood. Light is centred on the large foreheads of new-born infants, on naked bodies in the cradle (*A Labourer's Christmas, Little Nativity, Flight into Egypt*), on those comic little playthings whom mothers and elder sisters cuddle, making them dance on their knees. Close to the soil, sitting or standing by the doors of caravans, small boys and small girls mix with the grown-ups who are often no bigger than themselves, being mostly dwarfs or cripples.

No matter what their source of inspiration, there is nothing of the anecdote about these plates. Their figures, seated or standing, almost invariably show a predominance of that which is permanent over elements fleeting and transient.

57

Even in plates with the greatest variety, such as *The Crucifixion*, where twenty-three persons are brought together in one group, the engraver's sense of structure enables him to impose a lasting majesty upon his cast. The smallest details are regulated with unshakeable authority. It is from this combination of discipline and great pathos that Naudin derives his strength. A sort of premeditation, which shows itself in his use of acid just as much as in the drafting of his design, lends both weight and significance to Naudin's art. These plates to which we are referring, with the exception of the illustrations made for *The Man Who Lost His Shadow* (1913), *The Nephew of Rameau* (1924), and *L'Ingénu* (1927) are almost all prior to 1914 and scarcely outnumber fifty. They are slowly conceived, and worked at intervals of several years, with the burin introduced as a final touch, a means of colouring rather than an element of construction, used like the dry point to break down excessive uniformity. Only a few impressions have been made of them. Like Whistler, Buhot, and Forain, Naudin often acted as his own printer, grinding his own ink and choosing his vellum. He accordingly assumed the right of giving different interpretations to the same etchings, a practice which is perfectly legitimate when it is the engraver himself who presides at such inventions. His retouchings never show any abuse, and the supplementary effects which he seeks to obtain on the print are only a complement to that which is already rendered in the plate.

Such is the character of these plates that had their circulation been greater their influence would have made itself dangerously and widely felt. To-day, however, Naudin appears to have neither followers nor imitators, and one is almost pleased at the thought that work of such quality has remained sheltered from all that might have vulgarised it, as far away from publicity as its author was in his lifetime.

V. – WOOD ENGRAVING from 1860 to 1914

THE MISDEEDS OF G. DORÉ — A RESTORER : AUGUSTE LEPÈRE
AND THE FIGURE — HENRI RIVIÈRE

As long ago as 1852 the Goncourts, sighing for the charming wood-cuts of the romantic school, were deploring the death of this grand art before the onslaught of the etcher's skill. An article in *L'Image* by Raymond Bouyer summarizes the accomplished evolution : " What imperceptible transition was it that caused the formula of black and white drawing to give way to that of colour work ? We always find that an original by Porret, following word by word the written line, enhancing the decoration of a book, falls away and succumbs before the more ambitious interpretation that ventures to struggle trickily with wash-drawing and the stump. The engraver becomes elated and the engraving deteriorates. The simple wood-cut holds its own against all affectednesses, all calumnies. Progress and Decadence. The name of a single illustrator dominates the new conquest : Gustave Doré. "

In the past Rouget, Lavieille, Lavoignat, faithfully following in the footsteps of Daumier, as of Gavarni and Raffet, had drawn on the same block with the pen ; now the interpreters of Doré-Pisan, Pannemaker, Gusman, Perrichon — all supreme technicians, embellish, as actors of the Italian Comedy, the canvas prepared by Doré. The wood-cut takes unexpected proportions, breaks away from the letterpress, claims the printed page itself. The more it finds self-expression on an expansive surface, the more it follows after the effects of the theatre. Burty in 1864 (*à propos Don Quixote*) wrote : " It is not the contemporary engravers who are our accusers, but above all the methods of certain draughtsmen. We know of all the skill, the audacity, the ability that exist to-day in the schools of engraving, and it is just these qualities that seem to constrain them wrongly to apply their talent. " And Burty set delightful Edmond Morin against Doré, Morin, whose fanciful brilliancy, aided by that fine interpreter Joliet, makes revel in *Le Monde Illustré*, avoiding contrasts and overloadings, and obtaining the most subtle effects by means of employing plain whites. Events were only to confirm the lack of harmony between orthodox painters — who became more and more chary of committing their designs to the engraver's plate — and the experts anxious to compete with the copper-plate engraver or the photographer. " What is lacking to-day in the French School, " enunciated Burty in 1860, " is not so much the need for skilled hands as for daring ones. " Likewise in 1878, the Viscount de Laborde contrasted the engravings of Holbein, of Geoffroy, Tory and Bernard with those too knowing interpreters who, without any pretence towards perfection, adventured into experiments as much in opposition to the very spirit of procedure as to its object and precise resources. Owing to an aberration denounced by Bracquemond as tragic, the photographic foundation is abandoned in time. " Colour, the unnatural child of photography, by its mechanical agency, destroys the strength, the high lights, the very spirit of the wood-cut. Instead, by the precision and sharpness of his work, the wood-engraver accentuates and varies his values and brings text with picture into harmony; divorce of the original design from its expression seems not only more and more complete but equally the same applies to decoration and letterpress. "

Daniel Vierge, whose virile drawings unite a sense of the dramatic with a sense of light-values, is one of the very few who, with Morin, stood out against the deplorable influence of Doré. He foresaw the work of the wood-cutter, endowed the word " Realism " with a new feeling, opened the way for a new enlivener, Auguste Lepère, who having broken away from the technique of others — an outstanding event after so long a period of time — gave to wood-cutting not only craftsmanship but artistic feeling, being an expert at the same time as his own interpreter. With an established reputation at the age of 15, Lepère, side by side with Langeval, Martin, Tony Beltrand, Florian and Paillard, contributed every day to the *Monde Illustré*. His first original wood-cut dates from 1876, but it was above all from 1886 onwards that he established his complete freedom from control elsewhere (*The rue de la Montagne Sainte-Geneviève, The Seine at the Austerlitz Bridge*, etc...). He soon gave up work to order, real hard labour, so that he could better express what he himself saw and felt. The work of the management of the *Monde Illustré*, as well as English and American magazines, had centred hitherto on the feverish production either of drawings of secondary importance (exceptions being found, however, in those of Constantin Guys for *The Illustrated London News)* or photographs transferred directly on to wood prepared for this process. In the case of a large wood-block, this was cut into eight or twelve sections, which the cutters shared out amongst themselves, to be reassembled later. A man would interpret a drawing in ignorance of the appearance of the original; " facsimile " was made from " facsimile " without taking into account either form or model, ignoring all the necessary sacrifices, everything going through the same band of woodcutters.

The admiration expressed for Lepère by Félix Bracquemond in 1881 could not but aid his advancement. Later, in a pamphlet (*Trois Livres*) which, despite its brevity, contains some of the greatest truths ever expressed on the woodcutter's art and the art of illustration in general, Bracquemond defines the essential elements that make up the beauty of the woodcutter's art : " A print," he writes, " should bear the sign of its source of origin, and should be capable of identification by the process that has served to give it its being, that is to say, a lithograph should only be a lithograph and a wood-cut — a wood-cut... The measure of the worth of a drawing, be it on stone or wood, is to be found in the amount of relief it holds... From the wood therefore I demand that it should be clearly cut up by fine white incisions, leaving a bold black as contrast... The overcrowding of the amount of whites on the print is one of the unhealthy symptoms of modern art. Contrary to the views taken by many amateurs and the majority of professional artists, I maintain that it is not black, " the splendid sable, " that is the foundation of a print, but the whites on the paper. It is indeed this quality in a print that affords a sympathetic and volatile element by the imitation of the luminosity it represents. "

And this is what Lepère said once : " All the originality I put into my cutting is perhaps a very small thing, just to eschew virtuosity and simply follow the indications I make for myself when designing my blocks, " and it was beyond any doubt owing to Bracquemond's influence that he pursued the development of his gifts. " In his progress Lepère turns from the involved to the simple, he soon learns how to tone down the luminosity of a drawing, to subdue every secondary or transitory value in order to retain only the essential qualities. " Thus came about the conclusion to abandon wood cut across the trunk, a medium which is smooth and strong as copper-plate, in favour of wood cut vertically which can easily be notched even by a child with a pen-knife. The main difference is not so much in the substitution of a softer material, like pear-tree or box wood, (for even on wood cut across the trunk it is possible to make very simple indications, as can be seen in all engravings before the time of Berwick), as in the way the wood was henceforward to be cut, no matter whether it was along the grain or against it.

Although new generations had the greatest praise for that technique of simplification which, with Lepère especially, produced violent contrasts, warm patches of uniform colours, and tended to suppress all intermediate stages, this should not lessen our admiration for the engraver in those aspects of his work in which he is, in spite of all, at his best. With an admirable knowledge of orchestration and as though intoxicated by being his own interpreter, he multiplied his gifts as chronicler-painter in the *Harper's Magazine, Black and White* and, above all, in the *Revue Illustrée* and the *Illustration*. *The Reims Cathedral* (1881), and *Paris under Snow* (1896) are real masterpieces in which this Parisian heir of the masters of the XVIIIth century, has displayed his restless and erratic genius, his sense of movement and of values, with the aid of truly admirable craftsmanship.

In spite of the prejudices which then prevailed with all publishers and book-collectors (who still refused to recognise any other legitimate process for book illustration except that of etching), Lepère enlisted the support of the entire corporation of engravers and brought new life into the art of illustration. Reacting against the excesses of this craft and what he sometimes wrongly called its mistakes, he stimulated young artists, like Lucien Pissarro, the sons of Tony Beltrand, and J. Laboureur. It was under his influence and that of Maurin, a friend of Lautrec's who has left us some beautiful pen-knife wood-cuts, that Felix Vallotton tried his hand in 1881 at plates from which not only was tinting for the first time entirely eliminated, but which are dominated by a tragic violence, with large poster-like lineaments, sparingly designed and contrasting with abundant spaces of light. As a result of that interplay of reactions which is so necessary to the healthy progress of an art, the triflings of the " Similists " were soon abandoned for the syntheses whose secret and whose freshness had been preserved by popular imagination alone, that unconscious guardian of traditions. The influence of the Japanese and of some English designers, such as Beardsley and William Morris, made themselves felt at the same time. Artlessness triumphed over erudition, and " synthesis " became a catchword of one studio after another. Almost simultaneously, Gauguin, Armand Seguin, Maurice Denis, and Aristide Maillol reverted to the oldest processes of engraving. Emile Bernard, a true forerunner, founded *Le Bois* in 1888, a publication which he printed himself, and he revived in the charming images which he often touched up by hand those ingenuous features which are to be found in holy pictures and in the volumes which can be picked up on book stalls. Independent from the professionals, a new movement in wood-cutting, of unprecedented variety, was brought into being by painters who were newcomers in the field of engraving and even by literary men like Rémy de Gourmont, the founder of *L'Imagier*, and like Alfred Jarry. Maurice Delcourt, Alexandre Charpentier, Luce, Bottini, Paul-Emile Colin, Vibert, Ardail, Nicholson, Laboureur, Huard, Jeanniot, d'Espagnat, and Jossot all took their turns, under the undeniable influence of Vallotton, in popularising that violent style of cutting which consisted of a contrast between richly-inked surfaces — solid or in contours — and surfaces of light, without any transition between the two.

Colour, too, had its say. Artists, like Henri Rivière, Guérard, Tony Beltrand and Lucien Pissarro realised the attraction which polychromy lends to printing (as did also the younger Beltrands, who owed to their father their sense of ornament and their art of colouring and inking). The influence of Ugo da Carpi's cameos and the wood-cuts of the Far East can be clearly seen in Lepère's *Foretaste*, which came as a prelude to the rich effects of the *Fête-Dieu Procession at Nantes* and the subtleties of *A Rebours*. Supported by Bracquemond, he never ceased emphasising the link which should exist between text and illustration, and he maintained the superiority of the wood-cut in a succession of prints — *Nantes in 1900, La Bièvre, The Tapestries, St. Severin, A Rebours,* and *The Fairs and Markets of Normandy* — shattering the fundamental prejudices of contemporary book connoisseurs. Together with Tony Beltrand and Roger Marx he was joint-manager of *L'Image*, which was founded in 1896 and united the entire fraternity of wood-cutters, new recruits and old veterans, in defence of the wood-cut, both original and reproduction. It was on the initiative of Lepère, too, that the great exhibition of *Five Centuries of Wood-Engraving* was organised at the École des Beaux-Arts in 1902. He also was responsible, ten years later, for the foundation of the Society of Original Wood Engraving, which succeeded the old Society of Wood Engravers. Its aim was to insure that the true formulae of wood-cutting — coloured or black-and-white — should be maintained in the printing-press, and it furthered this aim by organising exhibitions of original wood-cuts, issuing publications, and arranging lectures.

This movement of revival was successfully maintained both in book illustration and in independent wood-cuts. Jacques Beltrand, whose first water-washed wood-cuts were his illustrations to the *Almanac of 1897*, combined the greatest technical skill with noble inspiration which he derived from the finest masterpieces of the past, and revived the great decorative print and the cameo (*Faun Playing the Flute, The Labourer, The Old Tree, The River Beyond the Great Trees*). The vigour and delicacy of his prints, as well as his understanding of fantasy in ornament can be seen in a number of masterpieces, which were later to lend their decisive form to the compositions of Maurice Denis (*Fioretti* and *Vita Nuova*), and which show Jacques Beltrand to have been far more than a mere interpreter.

Henri Rivière succumbed at first to the spell of the Japanese designers who had exercised so strong an influence on many European wood-cutters for over twenty years, but whose influence, curiously enough, had borne so little fruit. Later he returned to the refined and erudite process of water-washed wood-cuts. He was attracted by every medium through which he could express himself — etching, lithography, and wood-cut — and it was in the wood-cut that this admirer of Hokusai and Hiroshige attained his best results. He followed his Japanese masters in everything — even in the actual size of the prints and the style of signature — and he rediscovered those subtle harmonies and subdued lights and shades which one would have thought to be inimitable. Brittany becomes transfigured into one of the isles of Japan, the blue-black waves have a flourish of white or lilac, the tern black of a rock or the splendour of a sail or a buoy are expressed in all intensity. While he drew his inspiration, however, from those Japanese engravers whom he so much admired, his power was derived from a delicate sense of observation and a profound knowledge of human attitude, with the result that he had the same freedom as Gauguin in his Maori scenes, or Picasso in his negro woods. His use of powders diluted in water enabled him to attain that dim transparency and freshness which would have been impossible if he had worked with aniline. By placing his colours side by side or one over the other, Rivière, who always did his own printing, obtained very charming effects which a number of French and English engravers sought to follow. Some sculptors, too, such as Charpentier, Carabin, and Pierre Roche, tried to imitate the Japanese in their attempts to revive the art of embossing on hollow-cut wood or plaster. Lucien Pissarro, in collaboration with his wife, engraved cameos after his father's designs, *Work in the Fields* and a whole series of charming little engravings which were published from 1894 onwards by the *Eragny Press*.

THE WOOD-CUTS OF GAUGUIN AND THE YOUNGER SCHOOL.

It was through sculpture on wood that Gauguin was induced to take up wood-cutting. His first attempts (1894), inspired by memories of Tahiti, were of a later date than his lithographs. Engraving on stone had taught him the use of glass-paper and those light scrapings which are also to be found in his wood-cuts, where some sections, worked by touching the block slightly with a thin needle, are in strong contrast with others furrowed roughly with a gouge. It was the same mixture of subtlety and violence which was part and parcel of his nature, and which revealed itself in this domain, too. We learn from Marcel Guérin that Gauguin printed his own wood-cuts without a press, and often even without a roller. A very slight inking with essence was all he needed. Irregularity of pressure resulted in unexpected modulations, in pigmentations which stand out in contrast with the absolute whites and the intact blacks. The first stages often present the aspect of shapeless maculature, while in the subsequent stages the still chaotic greys are brought out more resolutely, and the lineaments become stronger. In some cases one extra colour is introduced by means of a supplementary plate.

A new series of wood-cuts, of which several were later converted into bas-reliefs, date from the second stay in Tahiti (1895-1903). " I am sending you a series of wood-cuts which, with my eyesight steadily failing, I have engraved on the first plates I could find, " Gauguin wrote to Daniel de Monfreid in 1899. " They are, of course, very imperfect and of inferior craftsmanship, but from the point of view of art I think they are very interesting. " And he adds : " It is precisely because these engravings are throw-backs to a primitive age that they are interesting, what with wood-cuts and illustrations daily becoming as nauseating as photo-engraving. I feel sure that time will come when my wood-cuts, so different as they are from all that is now produced, will acquire some value. " Thus it was that Gauguin arrived at the same conclusions as Lepère, though the ways which they followed were different. Monfreid could not sell these prints, and made a present of them to Maurice Denis and to Maillol. Some of the wood-cuts of the latter artist (*Women Sleeping by the Sea-Side*) reveal the unmistakeable influence of Gauguin. Later Maillol's style changed, and he took to engraving with sparing cuts and loose contours.

Typographic ornamentation plays an important part in those engravings (title-headings of the *Sourire*) which hold the first essays of André Derain in their powerful grip. There are echoes in them of the Aztec sculptures which Gauguin saw at the exhibition of 1889, of the Persians, the Cambodjans, and the Egyptians. " The greatest error of all, " he wrote, " is the Greek error, however beautiful it may be ."

His was an exceptional work, quite isolated from the point of view of technique. Outline is sometimes achieved by sparing cuts, and sometimes expressed by whites. An arbitrary element and a heedlessness of appearances prevails in his composition, both in the proportions of his human figures and in his distribution of light. A reserved black often expresses a light tone, while whites produced with gouge or glass paper are intended to suggest a shadow. Human figures are sometimes silhouetted in black on a light background, while sometimes it is the reverse (*Love, and be Happy*). It seems as though the fine needle was used less frequently in the wood-cuts which he executed during his second stay at Tahiti. Those wood-cuts are more like lithographs, and remind one of the primitive xylography of the West and of the works of our iconographers. A plate like *The Turkey* comes as an anticipation of Dufy's *Bestiarius*. With these exceptions this craftsmanship, savage and caressing at the same time, defies all comparison. Coming after Emile Bernard, the influence which Gauguin exercised over a great number of painter-engravers was parallel to the influence of Auguste Lepère and Vallotton.

J.-E. Laboureur, who contributed his first wood-cut to *L'Image* in 1892, was one of the strongest links between the elders and the younger school. It was undoubtedly the influence of the later " synthetic " productions of Lepère that inspired the series of *Toilettes* and many of the small wood-cuts engraved with a pen-knife in which the racy and somewhat dry fantasy of Laboureur found full freedom of expression. Raoul Dufy, Maurice de Vlaminck and André Dérain, spell-bound by the art of primitive civilisations or by the naive masterpieces of Epinal, followed victoriously in the wake of Gauguin, Lepère, Vallotton and of the contributors to *L'Imagier*, driving their conquests to extremes.

Raoul Dufy, who was drawn towards the archaic masters by his love of purity in style, made his first appearance as an engraver in 1908, when he produced his *Friperies*, a series of small wood-cuts which were only published fifteen years later. He realised full well that all essentially popular art is fashioned on great models, and that the most beautiful traditions are perpetuated by imagery, earthenware and song : that untutored hands and voices are yet able to lend fresh vigour to certain truths which, without them, would become stale with convention. The lessons of Leonardo and Dürer are still alive in the pictures which have been coloured in the work-shops of Paris, of Caen and of Limoges, for the enjoyment of children, old and little. Thus it was that the customs officers approached painting fully armed.

Dufy's Norman origin was responsible for that tang of the brine which lent so much richness to the whole of his work. When he was a small child he lived in an atmosphere of navigation charts, playing cards, labels of colonial produce, boats cooped up in bottles and thousands of objects engraved and painted with childlike simplicity in the course of many a cruise. Dufy, however, was just as much at home in that legendary world of fairies and demigods with whom his friends the poets had peopled earth and sky, and he tried to make transatlantic liners live on good terms with the Nereids and reaping-machines spare the goblins of the fields, inasmuch as to show that there is neither a break between the past and the present nor duality between dreams and observation.

Twenty years had to lapse before the originality of *Bestiarius* and *Orpheus and his Train*, which appeared in 1909, was fully understood. In these prints Dufy appears to have borrowed from the style of those popular pictures in which every figure is struck with light in the centre, while receding planes are suggested by large parallel hatchings on the fringes. Here there are no greys except those which are produced by alternating whites and blacks in the background. The cuts are not crossed, and there is no superimposition of one design upon another. Dufy benefited as much by his intelligence as by his flexibility and power of decision. He grasped the full value of full and empty spaces, of reserves of black and of clear patches of light, which are balanced in responsive harmony and allow us to rest our eyes, dazzled by the interplay of hatchings. He was fond of leaving traces of the tools he used, and of deriving delicious effects from rough handiwork. Never had hands so civilised prepared a feast so full of rustic savour. Never did a man of the cities revert with greater ease to his prototype of the woods.

The striking diversity of those great equal rectangles, featuring creatures as opposed as the pachyderm and the flea, succeeded at long last in finding recognition among book collectors. Matter and spirit, the true and the arbitrary, ingenuity and innocence, knowledge tempered by the unconscious, constitute a balanced whole which loses none of its perfection in *Love* and " Peach ". These plates had been conceived independently of any idea of illustration, and their subjects were treated by the artist anew on his printed canvases and brocades. Between 1917 and 1920 Dufy produced a series of small wood-cuts which served as models for a whole generation of engravers. They were all, however, left in the shade by Dufy who, in reviving many old subjects, knew how to put skill to flight by his own supreme skill, to penetrate the origins of craftsmanship, and to come as near the truth as possible by forgetting that he was wise and not, as it so often happens, by pretending that he was ignorant.

*
* *

The first attempts of Vlaminck (1906--1907) were mostly studies of the South of France and of the suburbs of Paris (*Argenteuil, Bougival, Louveciennes*). With the ardour of a barbarian, he invades the countryside and turns the Ile-de-France into a land of cataclysm. He creates drama where we would only find balance and harmony, and lays waste the most peaceful provinces with fire and the sword. Black and white is all he needs to establish contrasts everywhere. He bespatters his pages with coagulated blacks. He has left a number of large wood-cuts which are to be classed among the most striking productions of the twentieth century.

Byzantine, Polynesian, and Gothic influences are mingled in the small wood-cuts of Derain, his illustrations of the *Decaying Enchanter* (1909) and the *Works of Father Mathorel*. La Fresnaye tried to find equivalents in engraving for the pathos of his canvases (*The Cuirassier, The Artillery Waggon,* and *The Village*) by developing a style of large parallel gashes. Jou, a forerunner of Daragnès, was associated with Bernouard in founding the *Belle Edition* in 1909, which became the cradle of many young engravers. After 1911 he worked on the lyric and picturesque illustrations of the *Opinions of Jerome Coignard*.

The rustic sentiments of P. E. Colin, expressed in his illustrations of *Philippe* (1907) and the *Works and Days* found favour with book collectors. Florian, modelling himself on Giraldon, made engravings for Virgil's Eclogues (1907).

There was so much enthusiasm in this movement for the revival of the wood-cut — of the true wood-cut engraved on grain wood which holds the first place in book illustration — that although the War curbed its impulse, it was the first to rise again from the ashes, in all the various forms of its craftsmanship, soon after the Armistice was signed.

VI. – ORIGINAL PRINTS
FROM 1914 TO THE PRESENT DAY

A REVIVAL OF THE WOOD-CUT

One has to admit that the state of original engraving in 1914 was far from brilliant. There was nothing to recall that magnificent development which began with Manet and Degas and continued with Carrière, Gauguin, and Lautrec, steadily progressing until the opening years of the twentieth century. One by one, painters and publishers gave up their efforts, despairing of the little encouragement that was given them. The great achievements in lithography which had been witnessed in the studios of Lemercier and Clot were not followed up. Besnard, Forain, and Naudin were alone in making some genuine new contributions on copper. Helleu's dry-points, which had been so full of nervous temperament, degenerated into slipshod mannerism. Coloured etchings held the field. The exhibitions of the Society of Painter-Engravers became rarer and rarer, and although their principles were still faithfully maintained by Beltrand, Béjot, P. L. Moreau, and others, the absence of great sculptors and painters was cruelly felt. The best illustrated albums, published at their own risk by Vollard and Fleury, were sold at reduced prices, and the majority of libraries and book collectors were hostile to any spirit of innovation. The young painters, on the other hand, were all astir with new theories and colour research, and found little time to spare for graphic art : good drawings, indeed, were as rare at that period as good prints. One process alone still seemed to enjoy some favour with the younger generation, and that was the wood-cut. We have seen the attraction it had for Laboureur, Dufy, Derain, and Vlaminck. Beginning from 1917 and 1918, there was a distinct revival of this art, especially in book illustration. *Le Bestiaire* soon provided a fine example of this revival, as well as Dufy's illustrations to the *Martial Elegies* and the *Legendary Poems of France and Brabant*, and Vlaminck's of the *Voyages and Communications*. Emile Bernard, too, returned to the process which he was one of the first to put back into its place of honour (*Les Fleurs du Mal, Ronsard, François Villon*). The pantheism of Gabriel Belot finds full expression in the *Ile Saint Louis* (1917). The romantic flair of Jou, a master of the printing-press, was responsible for more than twenty of those riotous wood-cuts, full of deadly grimace, in which his Catalan extremism and whimsicality freely asserted itself. New illustrators grew to full stature by the side of their elders : Hermann Paul, Vettiner, Perrichon, Ouvré, Paul Véra, Méheut, Deslinières, Louis Bouquet, Carlègle, Siméon, La Fresnaye, Dethomas, Jean Marchand, Pascin, Othon Friesz, Le Meilleur, Morin-Jean, Quillivic, R. Grillon, Cochet, Le Breton, Boulaire, P. Noury, Thiollière, Max Vox, Gallien Sauvage, André Lhote, Baudier, and others. Some of them favoured the romantic style while others preferred the archaic, and yet they all helped to create a bond of union between works widely different in their ingenious variations. The inborn sense of ornament of the Flemings, the Poles, and the Russians enabled Masseral, Lebedeff, Tytgat, Hermine

David, Balgley, and Sonia Lewiska to take part in the movement. Wood-cuts flooded the market till about 1925, and they came in such profusion that a little sifting became necessary. There was not a young girl who had not scratched a piece of pear-tree, gouge in hand. The fashion was all for large masses of uniform colour, for easy contrasts of black and white, for syntheses based on cut-and-dried formulae.

These excesses met with the reaction of many of the painters named above, who made use of more accomplished instruments. The old vellum was put back into its place of honour by Galanis, Daragnès, and Siméon. Jacques Beltrand in his cameo plates and his interpretations of Maurice Denis, and all the seniors who exhibited their works in the Society of Engravers on Wood (Lucien Pissarro, Perrichon, R. E. Colin, P. Gusman) never wavered in their spirited defence of the glorious traditions to which the younger artists were soon to return. Simeon, relying on the support of Lepère, produced marked wood-cuts, such as *Jean des Figues, My Uncle Benjamin,* and *The Goat With Golden Legs,* in which he expressed many fine points which ten years earlier would probably have been condemned. Ornament was revived by Alfred Latour. Many book collectors, on the other hand, considered as masterpieces those works of Schmied in which he was so lavish with black, purple, and gold, as though seeking to outvie the miniaturists and the artists of the old illuminated manuscripts. Water-washed wood-cuts, abandoned since the days of Henri Rivière, were brought back to favour by Chadel. Among the newcomers in the art of wood engraving three names are outstanding : Daragnès, Galanis, and Lespinasse.

DARAGNES. GALANIS. LESPINASSE. ARISTIDE MAILLOL

At a time when improvised publishing was in fashion, Daragnès's first claim to superiority, as master craftsman, lay in the fact that he presided over the initial conception and the execution of his books, and achieved in his own person that unity of command which comes of being one's own printer. He began with a masterstroke by producing his *Ballad of Reading Gaol* in 1918, and followed it up with *The Crow, Mandragora, The Enchanted Hand, Proteus, The Morning Star,* and others. Daragnès could see that there was but a distant connection between the essays which he produced with his hand printing-press and the finished wood-cuts which were robbed of a good part of their richness and their candour. From now on, in his workshop in the Fue Junot, he would build his own constructions (*Tristan and Isolda, Faust, Susannah and the Pacific, The Children's Crusade, Eclogues and Mimes*), as well as those of his friends. Many of them took up engraving on the advice of Jean Gabriel, who got them their first orders from the publishers Crès, Dewambez, and Emile Paul at the time when he was managing the great collections at the *Banderole.* It is clearly impossible here to distinguish the artist from the amateur.

Jean Giraudoux, who saw in Daragnès's work a " confusion of inspiration and manual talent, " described him as " both the master and the slave of a great art. " It is certainly true that the purity of Daragnes's conception increases with the accomplishment of material execution. He possesses several of the essential qualities by which the inborn illustrator may be recognised : refinement, understanding of the text and, at the same time, that sense of unity which must prevail over text and illustration. This unity is always maintained in his works, even when in his books he reintroduces paintings in the form of wood-cuts or copper-plates, or when he gives way to mannerisms or excessive emphasis. Our preferences are for his monochrome wood-cuts which bear the marks of the feverish and sharp movements of his burin, and represent his genuine sentiment.

67

**

Already before the War, in his *Palace of the Popes* and *The Hunt*, Galanis rediscovered a manner of engraving in black, and brought back the use of the "*vélot*" and sieve effect, in order to produce moulded and light surfaces on his plates. His series of *Four Studies of Still Life* (1919), of which one was inspired by a watercolour by Picasso, present a subtle orchestration of familiar elements : tables laden with flower-baskets, books, bottles, and gardeners' hats. The little dots and the fine nerves of his design break the opaque texture of the tapestries; his light comma-strokes give life to the dense verdure. In modern sentiment Galanis finds an expression for traditional subjects. A lover, like Braque, of beautiful arrangements, he endows the ornaments of the XVIIth century or of the Romantic period with the tempo of a Cézanne. These qualities may be found in many of the books which he has illustrated with frontispieces and illuminated ornaments at the bottom of the pages, and which, as illustrations, had an undoubted influence on woodcutting as a whole.

**

Born near the sea, a few miles away from New York, Herbert Lespinasse was brought up amid wide open spaces, in a fairyland of water and sky. He had often crossed the ocean as a child, but those cruises were as nothing compared with the cruises of his imagination. A friend of the sculptor Alexandre Charpentier, at whose house he met Charles Dufresne, and of the engraver Germain, who initiated him in the art of engraving, and a close acquaintance of Juan Gris and Galanis, he awoke to a life of independence after a period of cubism and published his *Artificial Horizons* in 1923. Summary contrasts and violent masses of uniform colour were still at the height of fashion, and great was the astonishment evoked by his vigorous and thoroughly worked-out plates, where light circulates through a fine network of veins, large and narrow. One had to admire the manner in which, without working one design upon another and without the use of cross-cuts, this artist achieved his orchestration, differentiated his planes and his substances, blended the solid with the fluid, the masts and the sails with the buildings on the shore, the sea-weeds and the clouds, and at the same time reconciled the conflicts of things visible and invisible. So it was that while so many of the young engravers on wood remained slaves of their liberties, Lespinasse found that ease of gesture and self-expression which he owed to his learned craftsmanship, a technique which had much in common with the transfigurations brought about by the collaborators of Doré, the only technique which was sufficiently rich and flexible to express his wonder at the pageantry of nature.

The title of a second series calls forth a picture of palpitating skies plunged into darkness, streaky and undulating, crossed by slanting rays; seas which appear to be tropical, where bushy sea-weed, starfish, and madrepores multiply the mirages to such a point that the spell-bound mariner imagines he is seeing mermaids passing through the shifting prairies. Absolute solitude prevails here, and the magnificence of flora and fauna over which mysterious figures reign, inspired by the tales of antiquity. Etching and dry point, of which Lespinasse made equal use, appear to be less appropriate for his imagination than that fine craftsmanship which he had discovered and perfected in the wood-cut. From 1920 onwards, the *New Impulse* (*Le Nouvel Essor*), whose annual groups brought together Jacques Beltrand, Laboureur, P. E. Colin, Grillon, Alfred Latour, Bonfils, Bouquet, A. Beloff, L. Rodo, Gimel, Morin-Jean, Siméon, Bruyer, Deslignières, Gaspard Maillol, Guillivic, Constant Lebreton, Gérard Cochet, and many others, and *The Society of Artists of the Wood-Cut*, where we find the same artists side by side with Ouvré, Véra, Gallien, Jodelet, Foujita, Malo Renault, and Ben Sussan, — helped to keep the wood-cut in public favour, a task in which they were aided by the collections published by René Helleu, Vollard, Pichon, Gallimard, the *Société Littéraire de France*, *La Banderole*, *La Sirène*, Bernouard, Crès, Claude Aveline, and Mornay. *Byblis* was founded on the initiative of Gusman, *Plaisir de Bibliophiles (Book Collector's Delight)* on that of Paul Istel; *L'Amateur d'Estampes (Print Lover)*, (1924), on that of Maurice Le Garrec, and the series of *Illustrateurs du Livre (Book Illustrators)* on that of Babou.

The *Society of Original Wood Engraving*, founded in 1911 by Lepère and Gusman, arranged in 1922 its second exhibition in the Pavilion de Marsan and published its second *Album du Nouvel Imagier*. Engravings on linoleum, however, and even simple stereotypes now began to swarm in cheap collections and, as Maximilian Vox put it, " the flock of followers continues its foaming course, and is lost in the horizon. " Weary of these formulae, artists and public alike suddenly dropped the wood-cut as an obsessing fashion.

And yet, alone among the olive trees of Banyuls which are so reminiscent of the olive trees of Virgil, in the shadow of the tombs and springs round which the nymphs and sylvan spirits still dance, Aristide Maillol finished his *Eclogues* for Count Kessler. This beautiful book, which was begun in 1912 and did not appear until 1925, may be compared with Bonnard's *Daphnis and Chloe*. Like the lithographs of Bonnard, Maillol's wood-cuts are registered by the paper much in the manner of bas-reliefs. What Bonnard conveyed by means of his modulations, Maillol expresses by the simple force of his trait. Otherwise everything accentuates the close relationship which exists between these two great works : the very subjects, the frolics of the nude shepherdesses, the shepherds and the goats in a luminous and composed landscape, that odour of youth which proceeds from every page, that art of caressing a body as though it were a ripe fruit or a Grecian urn, and finally that ease with which painter and sculptor alike rediscover the emotions of an artificial archaism. Maillol was yet to illustrate, much in the same sentiment, *Daphnis* (1938) and the *Art of Love*, where large wood-cuts alternate with lithographs. Thus it is that this handsome old man who looks as gnarled as a vine-branch is almost the only artist of to-day for whom the wood-cut is a process still in its youth.

VII. – FOUNDATION OF THE INDEPENDENT PAINTER-ENGRAVERS

THE REVIVAL OF LITHOGRAPHY
CHARLES GUÉRIN. DUFY. PASCIN.

The awakening of lithography, that Sleeping Beauty, whose first appearance was made in the years immediately following the War, was a great asset to book production. We may congratulate the publishers who, in spite of the exclusive standards laid down by Bracquemond, realised that there were other processes, too, by which the presentation of a text and its understanding by the public may benefit. Book collecting has some good sides to it after all, since a number of artits would never have thought of taking up engraving had they not been introduced to a technique which seemed from afar to be full of snares, and which they yet practice to-day without any thought of illustration but for their own sheer pleasure.

We should emphasise here the important part played by the young society of *Independent Painter-Engravers*, founded in 1923 on the initiative of Raoul Dufy and Laboureur without any intention of rivalling the *Painter-Engravers*, but rather with a view to assembling all new forces and creating a movement which, by the breadth of its scale, reminded in some ways the impulses of 1862 and 1890. Every year the *Independent Painter-Engravers* honoured one of the masters of the past. New recruits, too, swelled the ranks of the original members, composed of elements that had not yet been adopted by the *Painter-Engravers*, such as La Fresnaye, Laboureur, Galanis, Daragnès, Friesz, Matisse, Bonnard, Roussel, Braque, Picasso, Segonzac, Raoul Dufy, Boussingault, Vlaminck, Frelaut, Dufresne, Pascin, Luc-Albert Moreau, Marie Laurencin, Vergésarrat, Leopold Lévy, Kayser, Coubine, Chagal, Lespinasse, Jacques Villon, and later Hermine David, Goerz, Lurçat, Waroquier, Gromaire, and others.

With the first exhibitions of the *Independent Painter-Engravers* we witness a revival of lithography, heralded by the publication of *Fêtes Galantes* (Ch. Guérin), *The Marshes* (La Fresnaye), *A Picture of Venal Love* (L.-A. Moreau), *Pictures of the Race-Course and the Hunt* (Boussingault), *the Full-Bodied Devil* (Vlaminck), *The Assassinated Poet* (Raoul Dufy), and *Serpent* (Jean Marchand) — all published between 1919 and 1925. Many of these artsits were renegades from the wood-cut, to which a Dufy and a Véra remained for ever faithful, while the number of etchers and lithographers grew from year to year.

*
* *

While still quite young, Charles Guérin was in 1894 put in touch with Duchâtel, the printer of Fantin and Redon. One can find traces of that chaste craftsmanship, as though whispered in the artist's ear by Fantin, in those little scenes, full of gentle, common sense, which illustrate the *Fêtes Galantes* (1919). Guérin's touch, however, is more refractory and somewhat frail. He is at his best in his vignettes, and has scarcely done a single engraving which was not destined to appear in a book. Although his habit of drawing with coloured pencils was, in a way, a training for making prints with several plates, Guérin does not excel in his polychrome compositions — such as the *Voyage Egoïste* — in which the design is slightly blurred by the colour-print. He has far greater skill in effecting transitions from grey to dark, and bringing life to a page by an airy commentary which does not weigh heavily upon the text and which preserves the discretion of a dream (*The Youth of Marceline, The Elegies, Daphnis and Chloe, Manon Lescaut*). These strange creatures, draped in a fairy disguise and set in surroundings which are somewhere between the realities of nature and the make-believe of a theatre, show a revival of the tradition of Watteau, Longhi, Monticelli, and Chéret.

Wearied by the lengthy process of wood-cutting, Raoul Dufy composed on stone his variations of *The Bathing Women*, transposed his familiar subjects (*The Paddock, The Terrace at Juan-les-Pins, The Plate of Fish, The Reaping-Machine*), illustrated *The Assassinated Poet*, and after executing a number of plates in colour (such as *The Sea*) by way of a prelude, made his illustrations for *Normandie* and *Tartarin de Tarascon*. As in his paintings, his flat colours do not fit in with the outline of his design, and the impression is produced that either the objects colour the space around them, or else that they are themselves flooded with light. Large pencil rubbings cover the stone with flat, uniform spaces which may be compared to the effects produced by a brush dipped in oil or water-colour. This arbitrary style is quite different from the attitude adopted in his wood-cuts. Here contrasts are not the essential means of expression : transitions become more numerous, and light-and-shade regains its rights. Dufy is at his best in his variations of the transparence and opaqueness of shadows, those slurring effects which can so well be registered on stone, and in casting to our feet all the treasures that are hidden in port or at sea : sailing-boats, barges, shells, fish, nereids, the horses of Neptune, — without forgetting that essential element which lends the sea both its movement and its colour, — the sky.

Apart from his illustrations to *The Marshes*, La Fresnaye has left us only two more lithographs : *The Oarsman* and *Still Life*. They possess an exquisite subtlety of value and will remain the most representative examples of cubism in engraving. We shall have to study the lithographs of Matisse and Picasso in a later chapter, dealing with the whole of their work, in which etching predominates.

The lithographs of Maillol, though they have not the vigour of his woodcuts, are remarkable for their fulness of volume (*Nudes*, illustrations for *Beautiful Flesh* and *The Art of Love*). André Derain published his series of *Metamorphoses* and made ornaments for the *Works and Games* of Muselli. Vuillard resumed the lithographer's pencil after a lapse of thirty years and produced four plates for *Cuisine*.

While the efforts of Ambroise Vollard were devoted almost entirely to etching, Emile Frapier enlisted the collaboration of Bonnard, Maillol, Denis, Rouault — all of whom had long been silent — as well as Matisse, Flandrin, Marquet, and Pascin in the production of his *History of Lithography* and his collection entitled *Masters and Lesser Masters of To-Day*. He it was who published the first series of Utrillo. New publishing houses — the *Quatre Chemins*, the *Galerie de l'Etoile*, Marcel Guion, and Petiet — were equally favourable to the revival of lithography, whose progress was advanced by artists like André Mare, Marchand, Chirico, Berthold Mahn, Asselin, Gimmi, Thevenet, Yves Alix, Vertès, Berdon, Giriaud, Céria, Max Jacob, Edy Legrand, Annenkoff, Berman, and Bossard.

Marie Laurencin was ever pursuing in her own mirror a she-devil without nostrils, playing at love or dolls in turn (series of *Life in the Castle, Summer*). Erotism is the guiding motive of Pascin, whose favourite subjects are his models, puffed up with indolence, sprawling over the settees of our grandmothers, with a vague look in their eyes and their thighs half-bare. Some of them look like little girls who were born in a shut-up house and have never wanted to go outside.

Vertès, a disciple of Forain and Lautrec, produced charming highly-strung studies of the types and ornaments of our time, both lithographs and etchings. His series of prints (*Houses*, *Playing in the Twilight*, *Madame's Day*) are very typical of the atmosphere of the post-War period, and he is the best illustrator of Paul Morand. Dignimont, a more popular artist, introduces us to reserved quarters. Bedon constructs his compositions in a powerful manner, as though every stone has come from a Gothic portico. Many of these artists practised lithography mainly for their personal entertainment. There are, however, three outstanding names among them, artists whose work is of exceptional merit : Georges Rouault, Luc-Albert Moreau, and J. L. Boussingault.

THE ENGRAVINGS OF GEORGES ROUAULT

The canvases of Rouault are full of beauty, but a beauty robbed of ease. His taunts, his cries, his grimaces, and his grating cannot be supported for any length of time. Unless one has a taste for martyrdom, one is condemned to live in close intimacy with images distorted with the hideous grin of Luxury, Imbecility, and Ugliness, in an atmosphere of ever darkening despair. The print is capable of greater secrecy and is not such an every-day affair as the painting. The print, which must be taken out of its mount when we want to hold it close to our eyes and to our hearts, can take in every manner of confidence with impunity. Goya proved this when he engraved his *Caprices*; Redon, too, when he engraved his *Dream* and *The Origins*. Never can such visions exercise a greater sway than when they are rendered into the language of black and white.

The *Driver of Horses*, executed in 1910, is Rouault's first contribution to the revival of lithography in colour. The passionate appeal of this plate is reminiscent both of Daumier and of Delacroix. A gap of nearly twenty years separates this first decisive attempt from the plates which Ambroise Vollard and Frapier jointly published. Wash, so dear to the heart of the romantic, plays a dominant part in these stones. The lay-out is outlined with a brush dipped in ink. Pencil and scraper come next, here and there softening the contrast between light and shade. The whole composition, however, is dominated by black, as fixed, guiding motive, both in the clearly defined contours and the big, dark patches. The whites, which are put in by way of contrast, have a wan and ghastly aspect, charged with tragedy. The stone is thus made to render the equivalents of those terrible reds of lees and blood, those sulphurous yellows and mineral blues, the conflict of which has been marshalled with so much enthusiasm by one of the solitary mystics of our time. Dense black and purest white confront one another, often without any transition. Almost invariably Death spreads its folds over backgrounds unbroken by a single ray of light. Here tragedy is ever present, both in sentiment and in orchestration. There is no dream that does not grow into a nightmare, no happiness that does not cast a shadow of gloom.

What are the elements that go to make up the mysticism and the revolt of Rouault ? What manner of vengeance does he seek to satiate ? What purpose lies behind his clownish and fantastic imagination ? Some of his lithographs (*Grotesques*, *Demagogy*, *Citizen Poupard*) are conceived as marionettes at a fair. Other series (*Mountebanks*, *Buffooneries*, *Travelling Circus*) remind one of the spell which clowns and equestriennes have never ceased to exercise over painters since Seurat, Naudin, and Picasso. Many of these piteous supernumeraries could find a place in a third cycle dreamed by Rouault : *Adams, Fallen Eves*. The idea of a curse is not only concomitant to, but actually precedes the idea of pleasure. There is an imagery which may be compared with that of the Gothic sculptors, multiplied for the benefit of sinners, showing a multitude of foolish virgins and all the beasts which hell is holding in store. Great ovolos enclose the planes, which are struck with light in the centre : bellies, knee-caps, shoulder-blades and great circles, suggestive of a glass-maker's workshop.

Two series consist almost entirely of landscapes : the illustrations to *Legendary Landscapes* (1929) and *The Lesser Suburbs*. Here, contrary to the majority of Rouault's compositions, in which the features of his men and women are distorted and their figures torn to shreds even when they are undressed, personages play only a secondary part and scenery is dominating : banks which have the aspect of trenches; trees so stripped of their verdure that one might think they were specially selected as targets in a war zone; blind alleys, cul-de-sacs, dark, suspicious-looking hotels, cemetery porches, and vague tracts of land. A little hill on which the imagination of a visionary has grouped so many strange figures looks as if it is only waiting for the Cross to be erected upon ir. What are the crimes that these fleeting onlookers lie in wait for, passing by a bleak, airless passage, or loitering by the threshold of some hovel ? Are they live human beings or mere shades, following in this procession of death ?

In none of his other works does Rouault rise to such a pitch of power, neither in the lithographs which feature the heroes of his great puppet-show — acrobats, umpires, prostitutes, — nor even in the interpretations of his own person — a redoubtable and tender Pierrot, embossed in *chiaroscuro*, wedged in between heaven and hell.

We should now await the publication of his monumental series entitled *War and Misery* in which, on metal this time, the artist has for many years been engraving his great testament. The basic design is here produced by heliogravure, turned inside out in process of composition, and further worked upon by every manner of instrument and chemical device : burin, roller, glass-paper, biting effected by the application of an uncovered brush so as to produce smooth or granulated surfaces and blacks of different intensity, without ever employing the artifices of aquatint. These plates were conceived over twenty years ago, and it remains to be seen if they will ever be completed. They have unceasingly been made and destroyed and re-made again, one attempt following upon another, as though registering the reactions which have been taking place in the depth of Rouault's soul.

THE LITHOGRAPHS OF LUC-ALBERT MOREAU AND
J. L. BOUSSINGAULT

Luc-Albert's originality is due to an unexpected mixture of daring and caution, of fullness and minuteness. His name should be associated with those of Goya, Géricault, and Daumier on account of that inborn sense of beauty of form which is common to them all. His stroke is impetuous, and achieves synthesis without effort. Each plate has the asset of a fine armature, a masterly setting, and powerful effect. Such generosity and vigour are moderated by the distrust which the artist has for his own work. A basic loyalty — both in respect of his model and his own feelings — and a love of order and clearness in everything act as a curb on his impulses, and we may observe the intervention of a kind of wisdom, checking the perils of impetuosity, introducing calm, and setting each object in its proper place, while giving rise at the same time to a number of hesitations and corrections which often cost dearly to the writer, and which in the language of painting are known by that apt word — repentance. When we glance at the various stages of the same engraving, we find that they reveal successive states of mind and show infinite scrupulousness of the hand, of the eye and of the heart.

One would not, therefore, belittle the value of Luc-Albert's technique by calling it erudite. The question is whether it is excessively so. Those who know the veneration which this painter had for the smallest every-day object and its significance, and his love of every detail, will understand how much he enjoyed toiling over a stone with the aid of all sorts of auxiliary tools, such as scrapers, iron filings, corks, and glass-paper, which he referred to as the " treasures of the housekeeper. " Never since the great period of romantic lithography had anyone taken such pains in giving polish to the picture which is revealed on stone. Luc-Albert Moreau could teach many a lesson to the professionals of lithography, for he knew all its secrets and all its subterfuges. Once again, however, we must emphasise that this science, acquired by daily practice in the glorious workshops of Auguste Clot, remained the servant of inspiration.

The artist has classed his favourite lithographs under a number of headings : *Boxers, Snows, Music Hall, Paris Spleen, Faces of To-Day, Aspects of Colette, War, Legendary Personages, The Poets.* But one is inclined to dwell on his more recent works, *The Funeral Dirge,* and *The Accursed Poets.* It is along with these, if one may say so, that a number of isolated plates of high standard has been engraved by him.

The march to the front, the return to the trenches, the picking-up of the wounded, fatigue duty under bombing, attacks, isolated agonies, corpses gathered in a row — there is not a theme which the artist has not experienced personally, not an object which he had not carried — equipment or munitions, all with their own peculiar appearance and weight. There is not a landscape which was not first engraved in the artist's memory before it was engraved on the granulated block. It is a microcosm in which every detail asserts its importance : everything has its relief in this monotony, everything in this washed-out world has its colouring. Some of the plates are aglow with a strange phosphorescence, lit with a terrible fire that consumes us. Others have a paleness which makes one shudder, or alloys of coagulated shade. We may admire this watchman of peace time whose only armour is his soft pencil and whose lithographic block is like a tombstone.

The water-colours and drawings of J. L. Boussingault, all done from memory, like those of Guys and Daumier, are remarkable for their elegance and dignity. These qualities arrest our attention when we glance at his illustrations in *Pictures of the Race-Course* and *Pictures of the Hunt*, plates whose ample forms and the surprises attending their composition carry the artist away to a craft which he is still frightened to embrace to the full. The large lithographs which have since been exhibited in the salons of the *Independent Painter-Engravers* strike our admiration not only by the ample, restless, and abrupt character of their design, but also by the originality of their craftsmanship. A kind of romantic ecstasy endows these pages, in which this uncommunicative dreamer seems to deliver himself of his secrets and his memories, with their brilliance and pathos. There are the spacious halls filled with silent guests, sonorous instruments (*The Sonata, Music*), faggot-carriers plodding along side-alleys, groups of hunters, gleaners, and grape-gatherers. Full of respect for the charming ridicules of fashion, Boussingault designs his *Girl Friends* and *Family Reunion*, in which his sense of grave humour and his cult of the wonders of every-day life strike a common chord with Guys and Lautrec. Other prints show the same old face of Paris, caught unawares in its most truthful intimacies. Plates like *The Railway Station*, *The Cabby at Night*, *In the Omnibus*, and *The Café Terrace* — illustrations to Fargue's *D'après Paris* (1930) — give one a stronger sense of the peculiar odour of the great capitals than any other engraver, with the exception of Bonnard and Vuillard, had succeeded in doing in the past. There is just as much pathos, too, to be found in his series of four lithographs in black, executed simultaneously with his black-style work on copper and with a series of small etchings and dry points (*English Series*, *The Champs Elysees*, illustrations to *Paris Spleen*). We shall later have occasion to return to these works, in which the painter, by successive strokes with the scraper or by obliteration, succeeds in obtaining, both on copper and on stone, whites of lightning intenseness which stand out in contrast to the mysterious, velvety warmth of his blacks.

REVIVAL OF THE ETCHING

In the domain of aesthetics, just as in science, one truth follows another. Or, better still, every contention is dissipated with the appearance of a contention of greater utility, and this last will be rejected, too, when its turn comes.

Like lithography, etching reappears in book illustration after the War, in spite of the discredit which had been attached to it as a result of the exclusive standards of Bracquemond. Arguments which were regarded as decisive had condemned both the separate plate on the grounds that it interrupted the reader, and the engraving inserted in the text, barred because of the deplorable indent which is necessary for its inclusion and the thinness of its lineaments, hollowed out by point or acid. In a word, it was considered to be absolutely incompatible with the type of print worked in relief.

From 1900 to 1914 the champions of etching could only boast of *Bièvre and Saint Séverin* by Lepère, *Dominique* by Leheutre, *The Man Who Lost His Shadow* by Naudin, and works of unequal merit which had been illustrated by Louis Legrand, Chahine, Jouas, Jeanniot, Huard, Hercher, Bruyer, and others, Towards 1920 we see a number of newcomers in the art of etching and the burin. They came individually, with no concerted agreement, and many of them had already achieved great successes in their wood-cuts. One of the first was J. E. Laboureur, who published *The Young Girls' Lodging* and *Beauté mon beau souci*. Segonzac made illustrations for *The Boxing Match* and later *The Wooden Cross*, which were published in the *Banderole*. The movement had by now started, and new recruits joined it day by day — Marie Laurencin, Chas Laborde, Falké, Asselin, Mainssieux, Dignimont, Gromaire, Pascin, Coubine, Hermine David, Siméon, and Charles Martin. Renegades from the wood-cut, such as Jou, Galanis, and Daragnès, technicians eager for every recipe of every period, fraternise with artists like Brouet and Vertès. It was a tumultuous efflorescence not without its dangers, for we can already observe the reappearance of many of the errors of the past, especially an unruliness of image and the ever perilous invasion of colour and aquatint.

Fortunately, several of the great artists of our time — and many of them on the advice of Ambroise Vollard who, as one should remember, had already favoured the revival of lithography, — have enriched the book market with a large selection of volumes very different in spirit, but all illustrated with etchings : *Dingo*, in which Bonnard tries out his hand in the soft cut before getting down to his illustrations for *Saint Monica*; *La Fontaine's Fables* and *Dead Souls* by Chagall; *The Unknown Masterpiece* by Picasso and Laprade's *Fêtes Galantes* (not to mention works in preparation like the *Georgics* of Segonzac, *The Centaur* of K.-X. Roussel, and *War and Misery* by

Rouault. Other publications were to include *Bubu of Montparnasse*, *The Call of the Clown* and *Muscat Grapes* (Segonzac), *Ingénu* (Naudin), *Poetry* and *Sea Cemetery* (Valéry), *Fruits of the Soil* (Galanis), *Faust*, *Tristan* (Daragnès), and many orders given to Edy Legrand, Decaris, and Alexeieff. The important fact is that for several masters, like Segonzac, who had never touched point or burin before, these illustrations represent a new departure. (Between 1900 and 1914, a period very discouraging for painters who took up etching, a group of landscape artists almost unknown to the wider public came to look upon drawing as an art complete in itself, and upon engraving as a form of discipline). Gathered under the leadership of Linaret, an artist whose disappearance was all too premature, and united by a common love for the German wood-cuts, for Dürer, Cranach, Brueghel, and Poussin, there was a coterie of impassioned engravers consisting of Charles Heyman, Kayser, Vergésarrat, and Leopold Levy, who in 1908 began their far-reaching analytical researches, discarding the artifices of biting and impression. They placed a craftsmanship of exceptional certainty at the service of a wide and restrained imagination. In their etchings, which are often engraved with a thin needle, they are fond of portraying the horizons of the Ile de France, and they appear in this respect to be forerunners of Segonzac. Vergésarrat, Leopold Levy, and Kayser, in their post-War etchings and dry points, reacted against that excessive precision which they had imposed upon themselves. They were out to find a greater synthesis and, by different methods, they succeeded in discovering equivalents for the effects of painting, always ready, after this necessary reaction, to return to their more rigorous craftsmanship of yore. Sufficient recognition has not yet been given to these very deliberate artists whose works, both in number and in quality, have been eclipsed by the greater names of Jean Frélaut and Dunoyer de Segonzac.

THE ENGRAVINGS OF JEAN FRELAUT

If, for the first time in her history, France possessed in the XIXth century a really good school of landscape-painters, it is because there were men at that time who were really athirst for solitude, who returned to the soil, embraced its rhythm, and turned their backs to the cities. Such was the case with Corot, Courbet, Jongkind, Boudin, and Pissarro, who all abandoned, to a greater or lesser degree, the surroundings with which they had been familiar in order to breathe fresh air, and adopted the attire of tillers or sailors, some strolling from province to province like tramps, others buying themselves strips of land or, one might almost say, strips of the open sky.

Born in Grenoble in 1879, of Breton parents, Frélaut spent his childhood in Morbihan, and made it his permanent abode for life. He began his work in that difficult but charming period when fame was slowly acquired, when calm reigned in the arts, and when engraving in particular was a source of interest only to a very small elite. He attempted his first copperplate on the advice of MacLaughlan at a time when the majority of painters were obsessed with the problem of colour. Few drawings were made, and still fewer engravings.

It is high time that in Jean Frélaut should be recognised one of the loftiest and most independent spirits of our age. The artist's character, his integrity, courage, modesty, tenacity, and the absolute disinterestedness which is so typical of his Breton spirit, are apparent in all his works. Some have accused him of painting and engraving with too much simplicity; others, of being too minute and scrupulous. He has been maligned both for want of skill and for excessive finish. Frélaut was unmoved by these attacks. True to himself, he only obeyed the dictates of an inner conscience, as far removed from vain virtuosity as from the urge to

76

astonish his contemporaries. Alone, he pursued his serious and active life, far from all noise, money, honours, and grants.

The majority of Frélaut's landscapes, in which the effect of light seems so inseparable from the soil on which it is shed and in which human beings and the nature which surrounds them seem to be so completely at one, were the products of his invention. Taken by itself, every element is true and has been observed. What nature has dispersed, however, the artist has brought together in such a manner as to multiply the expression and character of his creations, and to arrive at eternity through transient objects. It was in the art of black and white that this great artist felt himself especially secure, and it is a superiority which may well be explained by a kind of natural asceticism, by an urge to eliminate the accidental and to concentrate on the limited surface. However delicate and chaste are the paintings of Frélaut, they have none of the intensity, the density, or the depth of those more enclosed worlds that are his prints, where the slightest indication asserts its necessity, and where detail always remains a function of general sentiment. Even in the most furrowed parts of his etchings there is never any confusion or excess. All that is expressed fully deserves expression. The engraver's tender touch has penetrated everywhere : distant planes and foreground, earth and sky, man and beast — all have been discovered and created anew. A primitive can work in no other manner. There have been primitives at all periods, and the word should not be taken in its frequently abused sense of awkwardness or faultiness of form. Van Eyck was just as erudite as Raphael, and Brueghel, whose work provided Frélaut with his main source of spiritual inspiration in his *Return from the Fields* and *Sombre Day*; though born a century later, he could be taken for a contemporary of Van Eyck. The same immense powers of application can be found in the works of Louis Le Nain, Chardin, Poussin, and Claude, in the drawings of Ingres and in the paintings of Corot. Frélaut comes up to them all in his sense of measure, his manner, in that intimacy so full of propriety, and in his care never to express anything which is not up to a man's standard and is not, as it were, intended for his use. He is endowed with the same spirituality as they were. Even when he does not borrow his subjects from the Scriptures — which he has done with exceptional success in *The Evening of Good Friday* (which strikes a chord reminiscent of Rembrandt's *Three Crosses*) and in his *Flight from Egypt* — there is still a religious emotion in his compositions, which all have the common theme of the noble and wild soil of Morbihan, its hills covered with forests and heather, its cottages laden with moss or snow, its roads flanked with pollard trees, its shores beaten by the billows, its thickets ruffled by the wind, its moors, its markets, its processions and calvaries. It is with humility and with that respect which he always experiences in the silent presence of a landscape that he pens the features of the passer-by, — the huntsman and his dog, the farmer's wife and her child, the reaper, the wood-cutter, or the fisherman. It was in the same grave sentiment that he conceived his *Potato Crop*, *Horse Market* and *Fires of Saint-Jean*.

His art is part and parcel of that Old Brittany which has been miraculously preserved in spite of all the forces that could have weakened her character. It is a land where, as Renan put it, " joy itself is a little sad. " There is, however, a breath of heroism about it, and an odour of legend. Its heaths, its underwoods, and even its very stones have a gentleness that cannot be found elsewhere. All this intimate poetry, age-old and only dimly heard, is expressed by Frélaut in his work, where composition is guided by a native instinct and by an exceptional alliance of refinement and grandeur. To get to love this work it is necessary to go beyond appearances, to sink slowly into the heart of things, and to perceive that which is infinite even in the finite itself.

THE ENGRAVINGS OF SEGONZAC

In 1910 Segonzac had never yet touched a copper plate. To-day his work amounts to nearly eight hundred engravings. The *script of engraving* has become for him as natural as the other form of script.

The small rectangular pieces of copper over which his point runs freely do not seem to him to be a more cumbersome type of luggage than the sheets of bristol paper which he takes with him on his journeys to the woods or in the midst of men. Segonzac engraves in the open fields and in the halls of the theatres with the same ease as if he were expressing himself on paper. His method has been a source of astonishment to all those who tend to look upon *taille-douce* as a mysterious practice, and his art of penumbra is an incessant struggle against the elements — exacting patience, full of returns and discoveries — foreseen and unforeseen — and improvements.

He belongs to a great family of inspired and fearless masters who, from their very first attempts on copper or stone, possessed all the secrets of the craft. Claude Lorrain, Van Dyck, Canaletto, Goya, Daumier, Jongkind, and Rodin — they represent a series of impulses which are not in themselves sufficient to be the making of an engraver, but which were nevertheless bestowed upon many great engravers as a bounty from heaven : a transport of the heart which is transmitted to the hand and to the point, making it an instrument so receptive and a conductor so good that this slender and penetrating object becomes, as it were, a continuation of the nervous system. Through the point the nervous current passes into the metal and creates a miracle : an energy which communicates itself to the proofs with the aid of ink without losing any of its potential faculties of multiplication. It would be impossible to stress this dynamic power too much. Though common to all the graphic arts, it manifests itself with exceptional force in engraving on metal, as practised by those whom we may readily call born engravers, and Dunoyer de Segonzac is one of their number.

His pen and ink drawings already held out a promise of his engravings and long before Segonzac was sought after by the publishers, enabled us to divine his future work as an etcher. As his pen grazes over the sheet of bristol paper, it gives the impression of furrowing a metal plate through a coating of varnish. His shadow effects, brought about by a feverish network of lines, crossed and not crossed, would almost justify one in describing them as cuts and counter-cuts. Very slight indications which suggest the vibrations of the skies or the extreme points of branches, are opposed to the accumulation of absolute blacks on the massive trunks or the thick of foliage, as profound as the blacks which came out in his prints after biting.

With the true engraver's intuitive sense of means and with an instinctive faculty of transposition, Segonzac never ceases to suggest both atmosphere and the succession of planes : accumulations of parallel lineaments and of feigned traits which, in their juxtaposition, create an illusion of movement and define the living elements of sky and water, the undulations of the soil and of the human body, the intricate maze of branches or of a mop of hair. Prolonged impulses in the interpretation of form are succeeded by brief spasms, set out in contrast.

His illustrations of *The Wooden Cross* (1919), followed by *Boule de Gui* and by the *Cabaret de la Belle Femme*, betray the effort of the painter in working far removed from nature and the uneasiness he felt in his first attempts on copper. The rudiments of the art were revealed to him in the course of a ten minutes lesson which he took from J. E. Laboureur. He immediately anticipated the technique which he never abandoned, and constantly perfected : a combination of etching and dry point.

His *Picture of the Boxing Match* (1922) shows, in its technique, a considerable improvement on his War-time etchings. The artist now knows how to moderate his passion. His ease, too, is restored, now that he is engraving from nature. One of the greatest gifts of Segonzac, the gift of rhythm, finds full expression in the *Picture of the Boxing Match*. His models move from head to foot and, without arresting this movement, he has surprised them in the most elusive gestures. In his plate entitled *The Swing*, outside the text, we do not know what to admire more, the impulsive attack of the boxer or the sure, supple, and flashing stroke with which the artist portrays his model.

The series referred to as the *Morin* series, dating from a long sojourn at Villiers in 1924, is a set of prints without title or cover, consisting of one nude and eleven landscapes. Happy in being part and parcel of nature and in contact with the soil, the artist rediscovers here that intimacy with silence which seems to be a thing needful for his greatness. Villers-sur-Morin, together with some other villages of the Ile-de-France, such as Chaville and Saint-Tropez, is one of his favoured retreats. He returns to it regularly, as a matter of principle, from a devotion closely allied to his quest for independence, very typical of his character. Many of his drawings and prints are variations of one identical theme. It seems as though Segonzac experienced his greatest emotions and his greatest wonder by a contemplation of the same landscapes and the same groups of objects, and even of the same seasons — especially winter. He has nothing in common with that *blasé* type of mind whose lifeblood depends on stimulants, on variety, and on contrasts. He has a sedentary nature or, better still, he is the type of man who loves going over his old journeys again.

There is a great serenity in his exquisite little series dedicated to the humid and woody little dell. Its picturesque message is so general that anyone whose emotions have ever been stirred by a riverside flanked with alders and willows, a small, crooked bridge, and a church looking out over a row of poplars with a village huddled under its protection, go away with the impression that their old feeling of pleasure has acquired a new meaning. One might have thought at first that subjects so simple and treated so often have exhausted their appeal, and yet the same miracle is repeated which took place in the case of Jongkind and of Corot. An amazing combination of candour and decision, beauty of means and the art of suggesting the maximum effect with the minimum effort have endowed these landscapes with a power that is eternal. Under his control and guidance the smallest signs are sufficient to differentiate his subject matter, to indicate the position of a tree or a stone, or to bring out the moisture of water or the sky. Everything has a breath of life and, however small the plate, everything has its grandeur. Like his paintings and his water-colours, these prints establish most perfect communion between man and nature.

As time went on, the only changes that took place in the work of Segonzac were the different grades of its intensity. Every time he found himself in the presence of a beautiful subject — of a subject, that is to say, which roused his emotion — he straightaway returned to the state of grace in which he had engraved his *Morin* series, with nothing to check the forceful outbreak of his joy. The years 1925-1927 were very productive for Segonzac. During this period Petiet published about twenty of his copper-plates, engraved after the manner of the *Morin* series. There is no need here to enumerate them all. Several of them may be classed among his best productions (*Tall Poplars, The Grand Trianon Seen From The Canal, The Statue of Bernin, The Drooping Tree, The Entrance of the Menagerie*); the others are just charming sketches.

These etchings, or rather these " bitten plates " have been submitted to very soft baths, the result being an almost wavy effect; tenderness is always combined with strength; a fine point, cutting into the copper with increased burrs, retains the ink producing velvety appearances. Sometimes the artist attempts to enrich his exceedingly subtle orchestration by recourse to the scraper or by working on half-tints and shadows (*Bubu de Montparnasse*). Still more telling is the effect when shape and light combine; this can be seen in a series of studies after models such as *Woman with a Newspaper*, *Woman with a Slipper*, *Woman with a Sunshade* and *Fernande with arms crossed*. These can be compared with other fine examples (*Jules Romains*, *Daragnès*, *Régis Gignoux*), not to mention such plates as *L'appel du Clown* and *Thérèse Dorny dans sa loge*.

Segonzac has several times repeated the admirable theme which he called *Beau Motif* or *The Farm at Aire*. It is a small farm set on the side of the hill called Sainte-Anne that hangs over the Bay of Saint Tropez. Through the cork-oak trees one sees, as if it were a lake, the sea surrounded by the Moors, and the slopes that drop from an olive-grove. The largest of these plates (the engraver had never before dared to cover so large a surface) is called *The Bay of Saint Tropez*. *Twilight* and the *Cork-oaks* are variants in a smaller size, silvery plates lit up by a diversity of lights and full of movement. In kindred key is *The Port* with trees blending with tartans, *The Beach*, teeming with oily figures, or *Sun Bathing*.

Relations with Colette and Dunoyer made possible without any effort the illustration of the *Treille Muscate* and the *Fourth Book*. This power of simultaneously expressing sound, colour and almost a faint perfume Segonzac shares with the creator of *Vrilles de la Vigne*. An amazing intuition, a kind of instinctive grasp of things, quicker than average intelligence enables them to make the same discoveries in these landscapes. Both are disarmed as soon as the feeling of directness ceases to uphold them.

At the same time it is the country around Saint-Tropez that from 1930 allows Segonzac to collect material for the illustration of the four Songs of the *Georgics*. There have already been engraved nearly a hundred plates, voicing life in the country, harvesting, the vineyard, cattle, the work of bees. I have seen the artist in the midst of the best vineyards drawing the noble peasants of the Var as they drove their olympic ox-carts to the wine-press. Indeed this is antiquity reincarnate. The *Georgics*, alternating between figures and landscapes, provide the most important of Segonzac's engravings, the sum total of all that was most dear to him on earth.

Six plates were made for *The Kitchen* (1935), but more than 20 plates, of which four or five are lithographs otherwise rarely made by him, are devoted to the wares displayed at the butcher's, the poultry man, the fishmonger. Among these plates in some like *The Calf's Head* or *The Fat Pullets*, one finds examples really malicious, one might say almost brutal in their realism. Their appeal comes from that sympathetic feeling for a subject that has already evinced a delicacy, such as the interior *The Treille* or *Bubu*, or the box in the *Appel du Clown*.

The album of eighteen small copper-plates called *De Joinville à Bougival* (1937) of which only a limited number of copies was printed, equals in beauty the Morin series. One even finds a new form of restlessness. A strong yet supple needle comes to the aid of the engraver, answering the faintest touch of the hand. A slight change in pressure or direction is sufficient to alter the tint of the plate (referring, of course, to colour). We cannot escape these minute engravings, filaments, picots, all of which have their special plastic significance and that forcefulness which emits the nervous current with which it is charged.

Segonzac's engraved work would not provide an example of strength and health if it did not show that powerful inspiration also clothes the artist's means of expression, and that technique is nothing without natural aptitude.

From the beginning Laboureur betrays with a clarity from which he should never have departed the spiritual influence imparted to him by Lepère and Lautrec. As we have already seen, one of his first wood-cuts appeared in the *Image* in 1897 : the album *Toilettes* had already betrayed his sense of anecdote, the half-humour and trained imagination characterising the whole work. Laboureur never abandoned completely the wood-cutter's art, which, in fact, enabled him to treat many themes inspired by the war, though gradually he turned more and more towards the use of copper.

His first etchings, bearing the influence of Whistler, are of the same period as his first wood-cuts. Successive visits to America (1903 to 1908) and to England contributed to his development. Year by year his anxiety for improvement, balance, elegance and neatness, which seems inherent in him, is pronounced in his art. He avoids anything which may tend to create a vague charm, hesitations or shilly-shallyings. He makes continual effort, always perfected, to eliminate any kind of vacillation and any transitory coloration. The artist found his happiness in extracting from everything that came within his vision a poetry of lines to which his personages, somewhat dehumanized, were docilely submissive.

This development was intensified towards 1913. The chiaroscuro played its part in the drawings inspired by America, England and the Orient (View of Pittsburgh). Now, with increasing plainness, his course becomes clear, that of regarding the print as something flat. Truth to him lay in a graphic, almost calligraphic order. His engravings are poems the unity of which lies in a sort of preestablished rhythm, and a balance cleverly arranged between geometrical elements. If need be, he could have used nothing but a square, a ruler and a compass. He is a strange, delightful architect, who sets down on his designs with equal pleasure all forms animate and inanimate, dispenses with the " level ", stiffens the human body into a synthetic attitude, though, in contrast, makes the houses dance. His engravings depart both from painting and anything unexpected in the etcher's art. They turn more or less consciously towards the art of the burin.

It was with the help of a few burins that he engraved the *Small Pictures of the War* on some English brass cartridge-cases. Laboureur's personality takes definite shape on the Artois front, or on the quays of St. Nazaire, in an Anglo-Saxon environment. Never before had he played this game of analogies and interchange with such assurance. Everything is ellipsoid in his *Camp Pleasures* : *The Woman selling Wine* is as attenuated as her bottles ; *The Fat Tavern Hostess* harmonises with her barrels, the *Black Dockers* bulge both back and belly. When a Breton sailor sets hands on hips, one might think that it is a ship setting sail. If an architectural order predominates in every one of his creations, this is never at the expense of charm or expression. Distortions of form or feature accentuate each character, but do not overpass the limits of caricature. Here is where Laboureur resembles Guys and Lautrec. His attitude towards life, however, remains somewhat theoretical; he plans the concert of his lines dispassionately, without having to curb his lyricism. His work too, from beginning to end, is developed with quiet imperturbability. Passion is ignored, and the abyss is avoided. Publishers and book-lovers when applying to this master of clarity, were certain that a volume would appear of which the distinctive quality would be typographical correctness. Plainly pointed, devoid of jugglery, these etchings and engravings attune themselves to the cleanliness of a noble character, and have a twofold appeal for us : through their own sense of feeling and their decorative nature. One by one he produced his *Young Girl's Lodgings*, *Beauté mon beau souci*, *A Woman's Dream*, *Back Door of the Music Hall*,

Counter-Rhymes, Susannah and the Pacific, The Silences of Colonel Bramble, The Portrait of Dorian Gray, and twenty other works. Simultaneously with these productions, the artist engraved new isolated plates, little masterpieces both of artistic feeling and economy of line, as for example : *The Plate of small Cakes, Strawberries, Asparagus and Radish*. Elsewhere we see him discreetly employing variations in water-colour and illustrating *Walk with Gabrielle* with coloured lithographs.

When he abandoned the burin for the etching needle, Laboureur found it necessary to cast aside certain severities. The Cubist vogue, from which he had at first benefited, was beginning to wane. We see him gradually returning to less formal mannerisms, to more florid compositions. The writing becomes less stilted, his people become more human, though Laboureur retains those qualities of conciseness and charm that are so much his especial characteristic.

***

When Dufy ventured into the domain of etching — a province hitherto unexplored by him — he lost none of his adventurous spirit and fantasy, though he brought it under the control of an entirely different technique. After a few cursory attempts (*The Bathing Women, Nereids, Portraits*) he stood forth as master of the copper-plate. For him, as for Laboureur, the art of engraving does not consist in opposing the white of the paper to the shadowy world of ink, but rather in bringing out his striking lines to the full light of day, and adding dignity to the sharpness and clarity of the plate intensified by acid. Dufy provided for the biting period, as he had already estimated the depth of the cuts on a wood-block. The page-settings of the *Fair Child* have ingenuity, an exquisite freshness, especially the chapter headings.

There is, too, something fairy-like about the work of Marie Laurencin, whose first etchings and lithographs are deliberately simple (1906-1912) and thronged with imaginary people, as though they were the accompaniment to the little songs she loved to sing to her friends. Her technique as etcher improved after the war, and we find a certain mannerism diminishing in *Two Spanish Women, The Young Girl playing the Cello* and in a number of charming polychromatic sequels now and then adorned with old-world charm.

Hermine David, who started as a wood-cutter, found in the dry point, applied to book-illustrating, the best method of giving expression to her eye for romance. The rumblings of Pierre Laprade resound in the illustrations he made for *The Loves of Cupid and Psyche* (1926) and *Fêtes Galantes*. He is the engraver of open windows (Naples, Amsterdam, Camaret, Buzenval, the Pantheon) and interiors where his childlike creations return to the environment of flowers and old books almost ghost-like in their appearance (*The Black Cat, Butterflies, The Child with the Globe*). Here is a soft point indeed that strokes rather than bites the plate. An exquisite meeting places silence on this recreated world, and a kind of sad enchantment weighs over its appearances. This poetic charm is suggested by the most ordinary things : a casement opening on town or sea, an ocean of grain, a town dreaming beside its river, a girl painting, a child absorbed in its work — here is where Laprade excels in his vigorous etchings, fraught with silence and visions.

From the poetic fantasy of Raoul Dufy and Marie Laurencin it is but a step to Charles Dufresne, who when quite young was a friend of Despiau, Frélaut and the Linaret group, and who learnt to handle all sorts of material. His travels in Algeria or amidst the flotsam and jetsam of the flea-fair, where prowled the shadow of Douanier Rousseau, were the inspiration for a number of fine wood-cuts and some thirty etchings, of which the oldest date before 1914. A somewhat composite lyricism allowed him to traverse freely both time and space, to mingle memories of Rembrandt (*The Presentation in the Temple* or the *Crucifixion*) with echoes of Rubens and Delacroix. (*The Lion Hunt*). Love beats among his recordings, his virgin forests are peopled by Venuses; the archaic feeling of certain plates, coloured by stencil, gives stress to the fleeting conversion of this unrivalled decorator to the cubist movement, without however allowing himself to be fettered by any fixed dogma.

Picasso evades all labelling — a quality which is both his strength and his weakness. His engravings betray the perpetual contradictions of a seeker who possesses complete understanding (to understand, however, is not necessarily the same as to appreciate) and who has shown that he could put his hands to anything. His first set of *Mountebanks*, published by Vollard, is a contemporary of the great compositions of the Blue Age. It is here that we find Picasso most fully self-representative. After the war, he flirted now with frankly cubistic compositions, now with little portrait etchings imbued with the sternness of Ingres, with lithographs that are almost ghostly reminders of the First and Second Empires, with satirical cartoons that might have been inspired by the author of Ubu-Roi. It was a stroke of genius to illustrate, as though it were something concerning his own life, the unknown masterpiece of Balzac where it is written: "You have floated undecidedly between two systems, between design and colour, between meticulous stolidity, the stiff exactitude of the old German masters, and the dazzling ugliness, combined with glad abandon, of the Italian painters... You have neither the austere charm of bareness, nor the seductive wizardry of chiaroscuro."

Nothing more characteristic of the genius of Picasso, malignant and stimulating at the same time, can be found than this set of clear etchings engraved with such complete freedom, depicting the painter sitting between easel and model, eye and hand controlled by his btain, in short, a study in the real drama of creation. A hundred wood-cuts give the impression of palettes that are human heads, of profiles that overlap. The illustrations for the *Metamorphoses* (title given for his own gratification) allowed Picasso to create at one and the same time new monsters, and to invent fresh labellings for himself. The quaintness of these sketches contrast with the amazing surety of hand with which they are executed. One must concede to Picasso, both in his work on copper and on stone, an intelligence greater than the methods of expression. Here is a craftsman of disconcerting skill and diversity whose one want is, as with so many virtuosi, a little more human sympathy.

One cannot be entirely silent on the contribution of the cubists to the art of engraving. Braque has only issued a meagre number of plates. Jacques Villon, that restless genius, blessed both in interpretation and intellect, plunged into a brilliant series of experiments which thoroughly revealed his innate sense of how to handle the cutting-tool. The subtlety of Marcoussis has been responsible for brilliant results (*Portrait of Apollinaire, The Woman of Martinique*). The ingenious Lurçat illustrated *Baroques*. In due course the technique of Surrealism has left its mark, especially in the case of a group of Anglo-Saxon painter-engravers, led by Hayter (*L'Atelier* 17 — *Workshop* 17), as surely talented as Vieillard.

THE ENGRAVINGS OF HENRI MATISSE

Never perhaps has a more violent conflict raged between engravers of the craft and painter-engravers than that waged over the etchings and lithographs of Matisse. The influence — favourable or otherwise — of Matisse, as well as that of Picasso, was considerable in France and still more considerable abroad. An analysis of his work in black-and-white will help us to understand the discipline to which Matisse subjected himself even when it came to the composition of his paintings. We find that, by a curious paradox, the most instinctive qualities of Matisse often came out in his brush-work, while in his drawings and engravings there is far less immediate reaction of temperament, and far more domination of mind and will.

Gustave Moreau, that great teacher, loved to tell his pupils : "*In art, the more elementary the means, the greater scope there is for sensibility to appear.*" Matisse often pondered over this remark. It was Manet, too, who once declared that " *to be concise in art is both necessity and elegance.* " We must go back to Manet, passing by way of Rodin (whose cursive designs of the last period appear to forestall the designs of Matisse) to find plates in which the essential is expressed with the greatest economy.

However childish it may be to assess the value of a plate by the extent to which its surface has been worked and by the amount of visible effort expended on its composition, it was precisely this attitude which was responsible for the opposition which these very summary engravings encountered. They nearly always had the appearance of sketches, and the fact that the number of impressions drawn was usually from ten to twenty was regarded as a sign of self-complacency. The critics failed to understand that these abbreviations (or amplifications) were in reality but the fruits of very lengthy research and successive eliminations.

Matisse's first attempts at engraving appear to have been made in 1903. In the main, they are dry points. A rugged, not to say aggressive, model was chosen, and this very choice was not haphazard. Any attempt at attractiveness was banned as offering too easy a manner of approach. This contempt for charm, which was later to become as tiring a convention as its opposite, was a novelty at that time. Cézanne's *Bathing Women*, held in great regard by Matisse, showed the possibility of attaining greatness even by robbing the human form of all charm. Matisse only conformed to exigencies of the aesthetic order : he claimed to drive expression to its limit, both in design and painting. Engraving proper, even more than lithography, seems to have been suited to this wilful temperament. Indeed lithography is often but a caress upon a sensitive skin, while a more decided attack is needed to penetrate metal. Even in his etchings Matisse often cross-cuts the varnish.

All his prints, without exception, have been done from nature, A rough outline in pencil, on copper or varnish, comes first; then the needle is introduced to give the first essentials, that is to say that certain lines are given great prominence, such as a nude body, or perhaps a face. There are no exaggerated cuts, no shadows, merely outlines. One's first feelings are of astonishment that such a colourist should ban the synchronisation of values and of inflections that represent the justification of existence, one of the most lively of all the delights of the etcher's craft. But just as in his paintings he shows his preference for flat tints, so he simplifies his method of engraving by reducing his plates — which are, as a rule, of rather small size — to studies in the relativity of volumes, suggested by traits fraught with restless agitation. It is because a pointed instrument is used that we behold so much nervousness, such keen perception. Pen and pencil could never have taken its place. Among the two hundred etchings and dry points, produced from 1903 to the present time, we are struck by the constant and beautiful draughtmanship and colouration. Those slow, light bitings preserve all their characteristic delicacy, and give these plates subtle and fiery quality especially delightful when it is united with so much strength, and often so much boldness.

Only two or three wood-cuts are known to have been executed by him in 1906. Beginning from 1905, however, he devoted himself much to the stone. Many sets are simply in outline, like etchings, but of larger size. Others possess harmonious qualities and show care to express the most varied themes, as though the artist wishes occasionally to prove, that "finish" — using the word in its general accepted sense — is for him mere child's play, as well as a pleasure. His folder *The Dancing Women*, published in 1927, is very characteristic in this respect, so are also his more recent lithographs, greatly "laboured," where he delights in contrasting radiance with body; hair, furs, pearls, display a really astonishing consistency. Such analytical will is indeed seldom found in a work which prefers to present itself in the most elliptical form. Familiarised by the artist with these processes of swift expression, with his foreshortenings, we find a certain heaviness in his compositions, and are tempted to look out for certain weaknesses and insipidity. The finest of Matisse's lithographs fluctuate between extreme economy and complete affectation. He knows how to select outstanding models, one stretched out on a divan, another on a chair, in the disguise of an *odalisque*, with elaborate coiffure, be-sashed, be-girdled or in picturesque foot-wear attuned to flesh or type. These girls, performing their tricks in suitable surroundings, rigged up arbitrarily, in set postures, are given no chance of asserting their own individuality by this uninterested onlooker at the play of minds. Even when he draws them at close quarters or surprises them in the middle of some domestic intimacy, it is in their bodies that he is interested, and never their souls. Hence a style of art far removed from that which delights more than it moves.

The conviction, the seriousness which attends the birth of these scholarly games, the unconquerable gifts of charm often unafraid to charm monsters, the obstinacy of an indefatigable worker — all these induce an interest combined with admiration which is continually renewed. A lay-out of a catalogue, arranged by Mme Duthuis, daughter of the painter, includes more than 400 prints to which should be added a number of small monotypes done between 1915 and 1917, as well as 29 etchings illustrating Stéphane Mallarmé's *Poems*, spiritual experiments charged with a purity and character " abstract and poetical, " as Mallarmé said in his " *Pages*, " reminiscent of the author of *Hérodiade*.

SOME ENGRAVERS OF THE PARISIAN SCHOOL

There was a considerable number of artists working in Paris who participated in the renaissance of the engraver's art, whose inspirations, completely in contrast to the French ideas of romanticism, coupled with a yearning for the colours of the Orient, combined French lyricism with that of another origin, which often afforded a compensatory influence. Faithful to their Hebraic ancestry, Chagall and Balgley endeavoured to bid farewell to the realistic and find refuge in the bizarre. Chagall, brother of Lillium and Petrouchka, mounted a moonbeam and flew above the world on wings. With the appearance of the illustrations to *Dead Souls* we are better able to assess his greatness. Be it symbolising *War and Peace*, be it conjuring up Ghetto life *(Predictions Old and New)* Balgley, nurtured by the Prophets, ploughs furrows in faces, hollows out eyes haunted by pogroms or visions, makes the copper live with a lustreless splendour.

Pascin the angelic, tempted by the Devil, has paraded his eroticism all over the world. Wood-cuts, dry points, etchings, heavy shadows, wood and stone appear from 1900, in numbers approaching a hundred, works that have a close kinship with Lautrec for sheer fire. Biblical legends and mythology (*The Prodigal Son, Salome, Bathsheba's Toilet, Judith and Holophernes, Saint Antony, Venus and her Attendants, The Rape of Europa*) alternate with little landscapes of the East or West *(Cuba, Tunis, New York, Paris)*, or interiors peopled by inert, backboneless creatures. A voluptuous disenchantment characterises these impressions often deprvied of their high lights by the opportune use of dull varnish or the adoption of a very dark tone.

Despite, however, the carelessness of execution, and the weakness of line, the treatment is so brilliant that an extraordinary feeling for design shines through everything and many of his prints, produced again and again on stone or copper, ally themselves to the finest examples of the cutter's art.

In Coubine's work we find discreet scholarship combined with delicacy; here is painter and fine sculptor in one.

THE LAST PHASE OF CONTEMPORARY ENGRAVING

In 1929 Pierre Guastella founded the *Society of Young Contemporary Engravers* an opposite number to the Society of Painter-Engravers, so as to give new talent an opportunity of showing what it can do in older company. These yearly exhibitions resulted in the coming together of Amédée de la Patellière. Yves Alix, Gérard Cochet, Etienne Cournault, Anthony Gross, Pierre Guastella, Joseph Hecht. André Jacquemin, Léon Lang, Robert Lotiron and Mily Possez. To these names can be added a company of guest artists selected both from the juniors, such as Alexeieff, Annenkoff, Bersier, Collignon, Jean Deville, Jean Donnay, Gen Paul, Hayter, Montandon, Roland Oudot, Touchagues, Roger Vieillard, Charles Walch, Robert Wehrlin and Dethnow; and from the seniors, such as Dunoyer de Segonzac, Foujita, Despiau, Goerg, Laboureur, Hélène Marre, Boussingault, Luc-Albert Moreau. There is no enmity between old and new groups. On the contrary, all the three societies have often made their appeal to the same names. Yet it is necessary, at each period, that an ever more daring team should work, as one might say, for a certain future, combining facts with fancies. Every imaginable style, as we have seen, finds honourable welcome at the Salon of the Young Contemporary Engravers, be it etching or engraving, wood-cut or lithograph, colour print or plain black and white.

André Jacquemin continues with keen persistence his school of landscape-engravers which developed unceasingly during the 19th century. Master of his art, he brings to it all his inborn qualiries of a clear-sighted Lorrainer, even up to those harsh features which are to be found in such examples as *Winter*, *Thaw at Saxon*, *Vaudémont*, *Winter near Epinal*, *The Sinner*. His surety of touch and his confidence arouse admiration, though these are times when one looks for a more emotional feeling. Virtuosity has its pitfalls. We may remember the dazzling splendour of the early engravings of Décaris for the Prix de Rome, with their radiant skies. This man, to whom, as Montherlant put it, work on a grand scale comes natural, and who illustrated in turn Ronsard, Shakespeare, Chateaubriand, Vigny, Barrès, dared to tackle huge surfaces (The Nuptials of Pasiphaé), though later his feeling of elegance and fine conception inclined towards hollowness; one became used to the brilliancy of compositions whose archaism was in accord with certain new vogues in our sculpture. The somewhat avid grace of Guastalla, founder of the *Office International de la Gravure*, found its best expression in the etcher's craft. Gromaire, who illustrated the *Petits Poèmes en Prose* made the copper plate vibrate like brass. Bite and cut are equally deep, and, despite their heaviness, his designs are full of restless tremor. A savour of legends rises from the *Farmyard* or the *Ménagerie* of Joseph Hecht. His sketch-books (*Animals, Paris*) betray all the vigour of a pliant needle. Goerg, affected by the masters of the bizarre, has alternated between the half lights of Goya and Jérome Bosch's fascinating precision of detail. The liveliness of Anthony Gross, one of the discoveries of the *Society of Young Contemporary Engravers*, parades his plates into a world of dancing lines. Hayter combines both burin and etching to introduce a happy interweaving of figure and abstract landscape in his drawings (*Apocalypse, City Landscape*). Mily Posoz aims

86

at prettiness. Soulas, starting as a wood-cutter and always remaining faithful to his first love, in witness of which may be mentioned one of his best and latest blocks (*The River in the Evening*), has recourse to the needle for illustrating the *Black Set* and for the majority of his large plates, of which the most telling are those describing his native Beauce. The burin, introducing a new fashion, has a tendency to look for vigour that finds swift emphasis. His temperament and that peculiar heaviness which nevertheless adds to his lyric conception (as with Péguy and Verhaeren) made Soulas proof against facile effusiveness and what may be designated as grand gestures, and enabled him to display a discreet passion. When he bites into the copper he imitates that fateful and religious act of his ancestors, when they drove the first furrow and tore open the earth. His solitary plates, adorned profusely with corn-fields or ricks, over which we feel the passage of sun and wind, convey to us a feeling of what is lasting and universal.

There were some members of the *Young Contemporary Engravers* group, such as Camille Berg and Robert Cami, whose personality did not become fully revealed till after 1930.

*_**

If the wood-cutter's art lies in desuetude, lithography, under the impetus given to it by La Fresnaye, L.-A. Moreau and de Boussingault continues to attract many young artists. Alix, striving after greatness, paraphrases Daumier, but a more sustained scrutiny of his satirical attempts do not impress one so highly as one might have wished. A graceful and sincere fragility emanates from the coloured lithographs of Léon Lang. The sensitive Bersier shows in his landscapes a cult for Poussin and Corot. The restrained lyricism of Lotiron, of Roland Oudot (*The Forest*) and de Thévenet is expressed in their delicate landscapes, while that of Annenkoff aspires to the pathetic (*Extra muros*).

Thanks are due to the *Young Contemporary Engravers* for showing the world for the first time, at their 1934 exhibition, the engravings executed by Amédée de la Patellière, who died at the age of 40, in 1932. Every landscape, every figure study by La Patellière possesses that luminous quality which so few twentieth century artists have produced, with the exception of La Fresnaye. The means he employs in his treatment of copper are exceedingly simple. Here every barn, each stable conveys a divine mission : haloes float over all. From the branches of the trees falls the shadow of a cathedral. All unconscious is the transfiguration, as with Delacroix or Redon. Here fact and fancy come together. The patient animal quenching its thirst in the shade of the willows hides a ravenous brute. Patellière's masterpiece is, with *The Labours*, undoubtedly his *Rape of Europa*; *The Lion and the Horse* indulge in heroic combat, *The Reapers at Rest* recall the visions of Boaz. The *Bathing Women* suggest memories of Ophelia. Certain affinities between Jean Giono and La Patellière brought into being the illustrations of *The Hill* and *The Phantom of Kinaban*. Beyond this his work comprises some small etchings, about twenty lithographs, many of which have not been published, all of which breathe a restrained emotion, a muted exaltation, and that sentiment of awe and veneration which is communicated with equal force to human figures, skies, trees and mere objects — a mysterious and magic power. The spiritual density of these lithographs is found in few counterparts of his contemporaries, among whom is to be seen so often, as a reaction against slap-dash methods, a fine scrupulousness of work well carried out to the finish. But what we miss too often is exactly that factor which gives La Patellière his power, his earnestness of feeling and that character of finality and urgency without which the engraver's art runs the risk of seeming to be nothing more than an exercise or a feat of strength.

EDOUARD MANET
THE GYPSIES

1

EDOUARD MANET
BERTHE MORISOT

EDOUARD MANET
THE BOY WITH THE SWORD

EDOUARD MANET

THE BARRICADE

EDOUARD MANET
THE RACES

THEODORE ROUSSEAU
ROCK OAKS

RODOLPHE BRESDIN
THE HOLY FAMILY

RODOLPHE BRESDIN
THE PEACOCKS

RODOLPHE BRESDIN
THE GOOD SAMARITAN

CAMILLE COROT

RECOLLECTIONS OF ITALY

Etching

10

CAMILLE COROT
THE MILL AT CUINCY

Lithograph

CAMILLE COROT
THE STEEPLE OF SAINT-NICOLAS-LES-ARRAZ

CAMILLE COROT
THE HORSEMAN IN THE WOOD

JEAN-FRANÇOIS MILLET
GOING OUT TO WORK

14

JEAN-FRANÇOIS MILLET
THE SHEPHERDESS

Etching

HONORE DAUMIER
THE ROBBERS AND THE DONKEY

Photo Hypérion

HONORE DAUMIER
A LITERARY DISCUSSION IN THE UPPER GALLERY

Lithograph

HONORE DAUMIER

THE DRAMA

HONORE DAUMIER

THIS HAS KILLED THAT

HONORE DAUMIER

POOR FRANCE! THE TRUNK IS BLASTED...

JOHAN BARTHOLD JONGKIND

Etching

SUNSET IN THE HARBOUR OF ANTWERP

JOHAN BARTHOLD JONGKIND
MOORED FISHING-BOAT

Etching

22

JOHAN BARTHOLD JONGKIND

THE TOWING-PATH

JOHAN BARTHOLD JONGKIND
VIEW OF THE TOWN OF MAASLUIS

Etching

24

Renoir

EDGAR DEGAS
SELF-PORTRAIT

EDGAR DEGAS
MARY CASSATT IN THE LOUVRE

EDGAR DEGAS
PORTRAIT OF MANET SEATED

Etching

EDGAR DEGAS

NUDE WOMAN AT THE DOOR OF HER ROOM

28

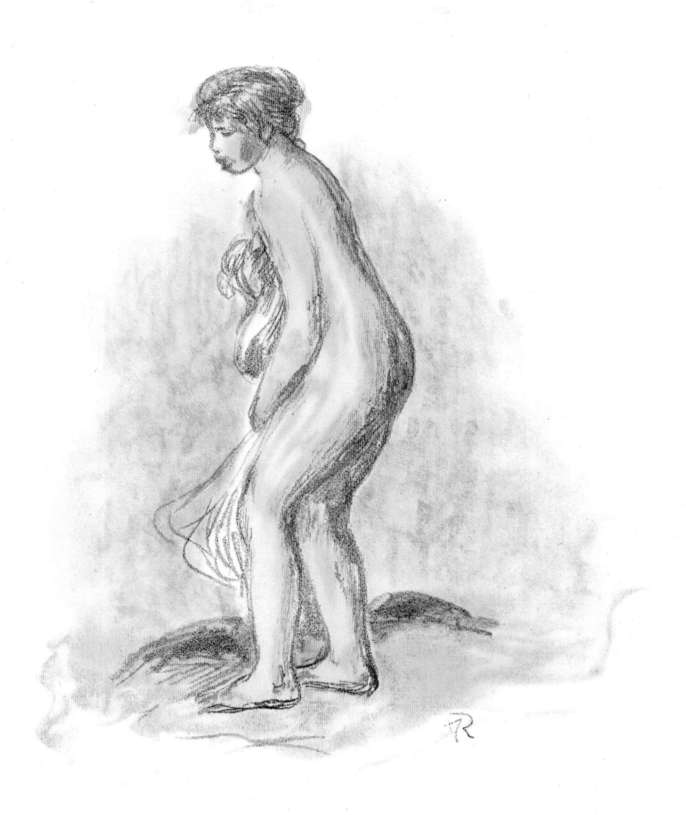

EDGAR DEGAS
NUDE WOMAN DRESSING

Lithograph

CAMILLE PISSARRO
PORTRAIT OF CÉZANNE

30

CAMILLE PISSARRO
WOMAN EMPTYING A WHEEL-BARROW

CAMILLE PISSARRO
THE MARKET AT PONTOISE

Lithograph

CAMILLE PISSARRO
THE GOOSE-GIRL

AUGUSTE RODIN
VICTOR HUGO

Etching

34

Photo Hypérion

AUGUSTE RODIN

SPRING-TIME

Etching

Etching

AUGUSTE RODIN
THE LOVES LEADING THE WORLD

36

ALPHONSE LEGROS
THE PLOUGH

HENRI FANTIN-LATOUR

THE BOUQUET OF ROSES

HENRI FANTIN-LATOUR

SARAH THE BATHER

FELICIEN ROPS
THE LACE-MAKER

FELIX BUHOT

Aqua-fortis

LANDING IN ENGLAND

PIVS IX
PONTIFEX MAXIMVS

CLAUDE GAILLARD
POPE PIUS IX

GEORGES BRACQUEMOND
PORTRAIT OF EDMOND DE GONCOURT

43

ANDERS ZORN
THE TOAST

ANDERS ZORN
THE CIGARETTE DANCE

EUGENE CARRIERE

PAUL VERLAINE

EUGENE CARRIERE
MARGUERITE CARRIÈRE

Lithograph

47

ALBERT BESNARD
THE END OF ALL

48

ALBERT BESNARD
THE SILK DRESS

Etching

49

H. RIVIERE

BRETON LANDSCAPE

Photo Hypérion   MARY CASSATT   Dry-point in colour

MOTHER AND CHILD

51

ODILON REDON
THE READER

ODILON REDON
THE FALL OF PHAETON

53

ODILON REDON

PEGASUS CAPTIVE

ODILON REDON
CLOSED EYES

ODILON REDON

PARSIFAL

56

12·3

HENRI DE TOULOUSE-LAUTREC
IDA HEATH, THE ENGLISH DANCER

Lithograph

HENRI DE TOULOUSE-LAUTREC   Lithograph
                                         « AU HANNETON »

58

HENRI DE TOULOUSE-LAUTREC
MARY BELFORT BOWING

Lithograph

59

HENRI DE TOULOUSE-LAUTREC
BRANDES IN HER DRESSING-ROOM

Lithograph

PIERRE PUVIS DE CHAVANNES
THE POOR FISHERMAN

AUGUSTE RENOIR

HALF-LENGTH PORTRAIT OF DIETERLE

AUGUSTE RENOIR
TWO BATHERS

PAUL CEZANNE
PORTRAIT OF THE ARTIST

Lithograph

BERTHE MORISOT
THE DRAWING LESSON

Dry-point.

'15 Mai 9[

VINCENT VAN GOGH
PORTRAIT OF Dr GACHET

Etching

66

ALFRED SISLEY
THE BANKS OF LOING

Etching

67

PAUL GAUGUIN
NOA NOA

PAUL GAUGUIN

MANAO TUPAPAU (THE SPIRIT OF THE DEAD WATCHES)

LOUIS-AUGUSTE LEPERE   Wood-cut.
THE HORSE-POND BEHIND NOTRE-DAME

Photo Hypérion

LOUIS-AUGUSTE LEPERE

ROUEN CATHEDRAL

Wood-cut.

71

Aux petits des oiseaux, Il donne la pâture
Et sa bonté s'étend sur toute la Nature

Racine

ADOLPHE-LEON WILLETTE
THE CRICKET AND THE ANT

Lithograph

72

Photo Hypérion

MAURICE DENIS
CHRIST AT EMMAUS

Lithograph in colour.

STEINLEIN
THE WIDOW

JEAN-LOUIS FORAIN
AT THE RESTAURANT

JEAN-LOUIS FORAIN
AFTER THE HEARING

JEAN-LOUIS FORAIN
AT THE THEATRE

SUZANNE VALADON   Soft ground etching
                                    CATHERINE DRYING HERSELF

78

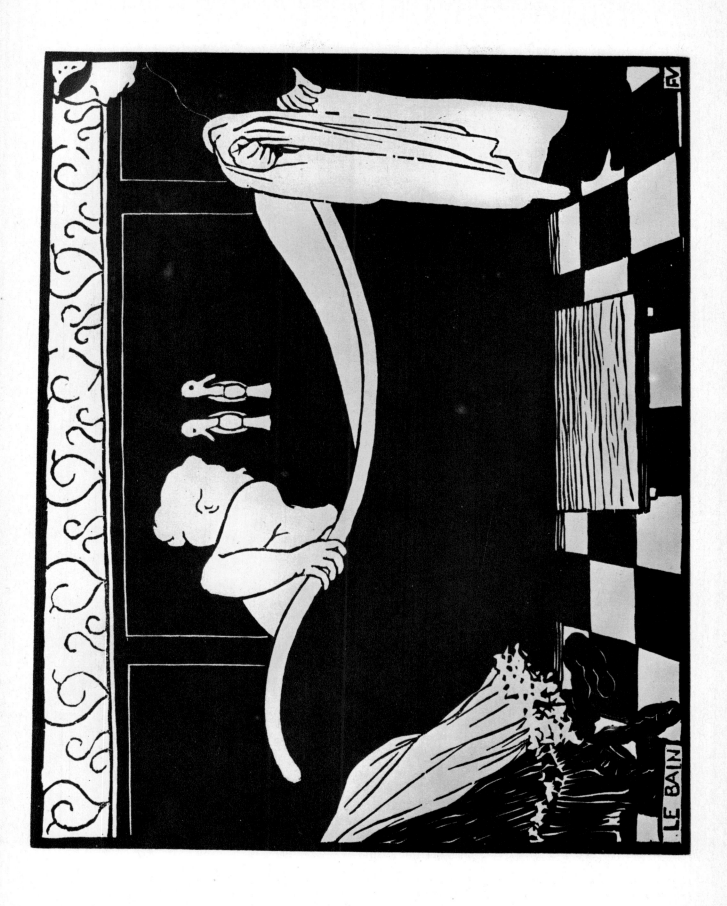

Photo Hypérion

FELIX-EDMOND VALLOTTON
THE BATH

Wood-cut.

EDOUARD VUILLARD

THE COOK

PIERRE BONNARD
THE YARD

PIERRE BONNARD
THE BATH

82

K.-X. ROUSSEL

Etching

IDYLL

83

P Laprade   Amsterdam

　　　　PIERRE LAPRADE　　　　Etching

AMSTERDAM

CAMILLE BELTRAND

THE PLOUGHMAN

JEAN VEBER

« WE CARRY OUR DEAD »

EUGENE BEJOT

NOTRE-DAME

Etching

87

GUSTAVE LEHEUTRE

THE TOWER OF THE « QUATRE SERGENTS »
AT LA ROCHELLE

88

P.-L. MOREAU
VIEW OF GARDANNE

JACQUES BEURDELEY
LANDSCAPE AT PROVINS

JEAN FRELANT

SNOW

JEAN FRELANT
THE FARM IN THE FIELDS

BERNARD NAUDIN
THE CRUCIFIXION

BERNARD NAUDIN
THE GUITAR-PLAYER AND THE CARAVAN

Etching

PABLO PICASSO
THE DRINKERS

PABLO PICASSO
HEAD

PABLO PICASSO
THE THREE GRACES

GEORGES ROUAULT
PORTRAIT OF THE ARTIST

Lithograph

JULES PASCIN

IN THE SALOON

ALBERT MARQUET
BOULOGNE HARBOUR

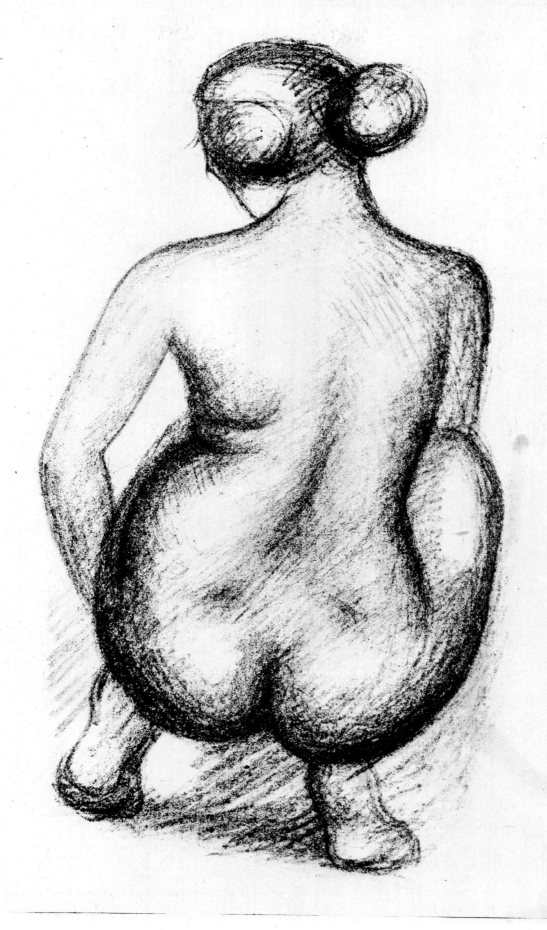

ARISTIDE MAILLOL

BATHER

HENRI MATISSE
NUDE STUDY OF A YOUNG GIRL

HENRI MATISSE

ODALISK

103

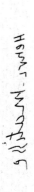

HENRI MATISSE
NUDE

ROGER DE LA FRESNAYE

THE OARSMAN

J.-E. LABOUREUR

TARGET-SHOOTING AT THE FAIR

J.-E. LABOUREUR

THE RECRUITS

107

ANDRE DUNOYER DE SEGONZAC

FERNANDE

Etching

ANDRE DUNOYER DE SEGONZAC
LANDSCAPE IN THE MORIN COUNTRY

Etching

ANDRE DUNOYER DE SEGONZAC

LANDSCAPE IN THE MORIN COUNTRY

ANDRE DUNOYER DE SEGONZAC

CORK OAKS

Etching

111

LUC-ALBERT MOREAU

EIGHT, NINE, TEN

Lithograph

LUC-ALBERT MOREAU
THE BOOK-LOVER

JEAN-LOUIS BOUSSINGAULT
THE OMNIBUS

Lithograph

CHARLES DUFRESNE
THE PRESENTATION IN THE TEMPLE

Etching

KAYSER
PORTRAIT

RAOUL DUFY

LOVE

RAOUL DUFY
LANDSCAPE IN SOUTHERN FRANCE

MAURICE DE VLAMINCK
THE OISE AT SERGY

Etching.

MARIE LAURENCIN
SPANISH WOMEN

Etching.

HERBERT LESPINASSE
THE HARBOUR

HENRI VERGE-SARRAT
WINTER LANDSCAPE

Etching

122

ANDRE JACQUEMIN
LANDSCAPE WITH FISHERMAN

Etching.

MAURICE UTRILLO
THE SEINE EMBANKMENT

124

AMEDEE DE LA PATELLIERE
THE RAPE OF EUROPA

Lithograph

ANDRE DERAIN
FACE

9/30

Verts

Photo Hypérion   MARCEL VERTES   Lithograph
ENGAGEMENT

LOUIS-JOSEPH SOULAS
RIVER AT DUSK

Wood-cut.

INDEX OF ARTISTS

LIST OF COLOUR PLATES

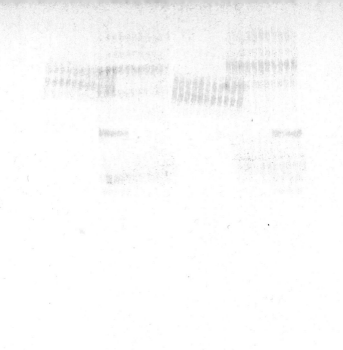